Test Item File

INTEGRATED ADVERTISING, PROMOTION, AND MARKETING COMMUNICATIONS

Second Edition

Kenneth E. Clow *University of Louisiana*
Donald Baack *Pittsburg State University*

PEARSON
Prentice Hall

Upper Saddle River, New Jersey 07458

Editor-in-Chief: Jeff Shelstad
Acquisitions Editor: Katie Stevens
Assistant Editor: Melissa Pellerano
Manager, Print Production: Christy Mahon
Production Editor & Buyer: Carol O'Rourke
Printer/Binder: Integrated Book Technology, Inc.

10 9 8 7 6 5 4 3 2
ISBN 0-13-141506-9

Contents

Introduction

INTRODUCTION

Welcome to the *Test Item File* for the Clow and Baack text entitled *Integrated Advertising, Promotions, and Marketing Communications, 2nd edition.* This test bank was designed with the student and instructor in mind. All of the questions contained in the manual are taken from the text. Therefore, the instructor will find it easy to explain the source of the questions on a test.

Each chapter in the *Test Item File* contains three types of questions: True/False, Multiple Choice, and Short Answer. Each question is formatted with the question number, possible answers, the correct answer, a difficulty scale, and the page where the question concept and answer may be found in the book. The questions in the *Test Item File* generally begin at the first of the chapter and follow a logical sequence to the end of the chapter within each difficulty level category.

Short Answer Questions generally address primary components of each chapter. The answer for each short answer question is provided, but is not always all-inclusive, depending on what is asked for. The instructor should obviously allow for additional student response or slightly different responses where that makes sense.

Each question includes a difficulty scale. This is intended to help the instructor in choosing the degree of difficulty of the questions and answers they might put on an examination. The *Test Item File* provides a mixture of these difficulty levels for each chapter, however there are more (easy) and (moderate) questions and fewer (difficult) questions.

Students taking examinations drawn from the *Test Item File* should be encouraged to carefully read the material in the text and should be instructed to choose the "best answer" from the available options. Because many questions are drawn from these sources, students should be expected to include figures, tables, and other exhibits when preparing for their examinations.

Good luck with your course and subsequent evaluation of student learning. Should you have any difficulty with the question content, please contact me at **Clow@ulm.edu**. Prentice Hall and I sincerely hope you find this supplemental material useful. Thank you for using the Clow/Baack text.

Kenneth E. Clow, Ph.D., Professor of Marketing, University of Louisiana at Monroe
Donald Baack, Ph.D., Professor of Management, Pittsburg State University

CHAPTER 1
INTEGRATED MARKETING COMMUNICATIONS

True-False Questions

1) In recent years, the nature of the job of account executive has changed due to new pressures in the area of accountability.
(True; Easy; p. 4)

2) Communication is defined as transmitting, receiving, and processing information.
(True; Easy; p. 5)

3) The large number of marketing messages consumers are exposed to daily is an example of noise and is also called clutter.
(True; Easy; p. 8)

4) The budget preparation stage of a marketing analysis focuses on finding company strengths and weaknesses and environmental opportunities and threats.
(False; Easy; p. 9)

5) In today's marketplace, advertising alone is often enough to sustain sales.
(False; Easy; p. 17)

6) An integrated marketing communications program should be viewed as an overall organizational process rather than a marketing plan or marketing function.
(True; Easy; p. 12)

7) Brand parity is a common consumer belief that many brands consist of or offer the same set of attributes.
(True; Easy; p. 18)

8) The person who directs the filming of a television commercial is normally the brand manager.
(False; Moderate; p. 5)

9) Television commercials, print ads, and retail coupons are examples of encoding.
(True; Moderate; p. 5)

10) Decoding occurs when the message is interpreted by the receiver.
(True; Moderate; p. 6)

11) Coca-Cola's consistent use of the same logo, theme, and colors on packages and in advertisements is an example of an integrated marketing communications approach to promotions.
(True; Moderate; p. 12)

12) One of the major challenges for marketers is gathering information about potential customers and product sales.
(False; Moderate: p. 15)

13) A Globally Integrated Marketing Communications plan creates a standard message across all cultures.
(False; Moderate; p. 20)

14) Adaptation in a GMIC program may mean rewriting an advertisement to fit the nuances of a given language and culture.
(True; Moderate; p. 20)

15) Susan researches car stereos on the Internet and by visiting Best Buy. This is an example of a shift in power to the retailer.
(False; Challenging; p. 16)

16) A Web site is not considered a contact point because both the consumer and the company employee talking to the consumer can remain anonymous.
(False; Challenging; p. 18)

17) When Nike gives a discount to entice Sears to carry its shoes, Nike is offering a trade promotion.
(True; Challenging; p. 11)

18) Bruce always bought Kleenex brand tissues until the past two years when he decided that all tissues were pretty much the same. This is an example of brand parity.
(True; Challenging; p. 18)

19) Television is becoming a more effective mass media outlet for advertising because so many more people own sets and have access to cable.
(False; Challenging; p.19)

20) Standardization would be an effective GMIC tactic in the Middle East because of the variety of religions and cultures.
(False; Challenging; p. 20)

Multiple Choice Questions

21) In the turbulent new marketing environment, _____ has become a primary concern to advertising agencies and companies hiring those agencies.
   a) accountability
   b) representation
   c) pricing
   d) control
   (a; Easy; p. 4)

22) The individuals who develop the actual advertisements for promotional campaigns are called _____.
   a) account executives
   b) brand managers
   c) creatives
   d) receivers
   (c; Easy; p. 5)

23) Which would be a sender?
   a) a company seeking to sell a product
   b) a television set
   c) sales data following a campaign
   d) a consumer ignoring an ad in a newspaper
   (a; Easy; p. 5)

24) Preparing ad copy is _____ .
   a) decoding
   b) situational analysis
   c) encoding
   d) filtering out noise
   (c; Easy; p. 5)

25) The items that carry the message from the sender to the receiver are _____ .
   a) encoding processes
   b) decoding processes
   c) transmission devices
   d) feedback devices
   (c; Easy; p. 6)

26) Noise is _____ .
   a) anything which carries a message from a sender to a receiver
   b) changing a message to match the specific needs of a region
   c) a verbal or nonverbal cue delivered by the sender
   d) anything that distorts the sender's message
   (d; Easy; p. 7)

27) Which would be an example of feedback in a marketing channel?
   a) new product development
   b) a customer complaint
   c) a decision to begin international operations
   d) removing a product from the market

(b; Easy; p. 8)

28) Which is an example of within-company noise?
   a) an age difference between the CEO and his secretary
   b) poor selling techniques in the sales department
   c) poor media choices by creatives
   d) poor lateral communication between marketing and production departments

(d; Easy, p. 7)

29) In preparing an ad, a creative is most likely going to be _____.
   a) a sender or encoder
   b) a production specialist
   c) a decoder or receiver
   d) noise or clutter

(a; Easy; p. 5)

30) Of the four "P's" of marketing, where does integrated marketing communications belong?
   a) pricing decisions
   b) product design
   c) promotion
   d) distribution

(c; Easy, p. 9)

31) Which is not a component of a marketing plan?
   a) situational analysis
   b) marketing objectives
   c) human resource assessment
   d) marketing strategies and tactics

(c; Easy; p. 9)

32) Which is ordinarily not considered part of the promotions mix?
   a) advertising
   b) product design
   c) personal selling
   d) sales promotions

(b; Easy; p. 8)

33) In this text, an integrated marketing communications program is compared to _____.
    a) a pyramid of marketing activities
    b) the parts of a computer
    c) the government of a state
    d) a car traveling at a high speed
(a; Easy; p. 10)

34) A typical marketing channel is _____.
    a) producer-wholesaler-retailer-consumer
    b) consumer-producer-retailer-wholesaler
    c) producer-consumer-retailer-wholesaler
    d) business agent-retailer-producer-business merchant
(a; Easy; p. 16)

35) Many marketing experts agree channel power has shifted from _____ .
    a) the producer to the wholesaler
    b) the ad agency to the marketing department
    c) the retailer to the wholesaler
    d) from all other groups to the consumer
(d; Easy; p. 16)

36) The competitive environment is now more _____ .
    a) local
    b) global
    c) concentrated
    d) benign
(b; Easy; p. 17)

37) Brand parity is _____ .
    a) the perception that there are no real differences between major brands
    b) the perception that most advertising is false
    c) the belief that all advertisers say essentially the same thing
    d) the idea that brands are distinct and easy to identify
(a; Easy; p. 18)

38) Mass media advertising _____ .
    a) is as effective as ever
    b) has risen in the past decade
    c) has not been assessed effectively
    d) is declining in effectiveness
(d; Easy; p. 18)

39) A contact point is _____.
   a) the place where a marketer reaches the production team
   b) the place where the product is packaged or sold
   c) a description of the effects of an advertisement
   d) a place in which a consumer interacts with a company
(d; Easy; p. 18)

40) GIMC stands for _____.
   a) Globally Integrated Marketing Communications
   b) Global and Institutional Marketing Concepts
   c) Generic and Institutionalized Marketing Creations
   d) Generating Ideas for Marketing Control
(a; Easy; p. 20)

41) In terms of marketing communications, standardization is _____.
   a) the same message across national boundaries
   b) a form of adaptation
   c) new product development
   d) a new form of the promotions mix
(a; Easy; p. 20)

42) In terms of marketing communications, adaptation is _____.
   a) not used in international environments
   b) a form of e-commerce
   c) advertising in unusual media
   d) adjusting a message to local conditions
(d; Easy; p. 20)

43) An advertising agency is told a campaign should result in a 20% increase in sales. This is an example of _____ .
   a) marketing myopia
   b) standardization
   c) adaptation
   d) accountability
(d; Moderate; p. 4)

44) Julie is explaining an integrated marketing communications program to Michael. In this situation _____ .
   a) Julie is a sender and Michael is an encoder
   b) Julie is a receiver and Michael is providing feedback
   c) Julie is a sender and Michael is a receiver
   d) Julie is a transmission device and Michael is a decoder
(c; Moderate; pp. 5,7)

45) A consumer sees a billboard while driving. The billboard is _____ .
   a) a creative
   b) a decoding device
   c) a transmission device
   d) feedback and clutter
(c; Moderate; p. 6)

46) Michelle is trying to tutor George, but a stereo is playing loudly in the room next door, making it difficult to concentrate. This is an example of _____ .
   a) feedback disruption
   b) noise
   c) encoding design
   d) a contact point
(b; Moderate; p. 7)

47) While browsing the Internet, a consumer encounters a new pop-up ad every time a new page is opened. This is an example of _____ .
   a) advertising effectiveness
   b) perceptual distortion
   c) clutter
   d) brand parity
(c; Moderate; p. 8)

48) Papa John's theme "Better Ingredients, Better Pizza" shown on all marketing messages is an example of _____ .
   a) a complete IMC program
   b) needless repetition creating clutter
   c) a situational analysis
   d) cross-functional communication
(a; Moderate; p. 9)

49) Microsoft's leaders have discovered the company's literature tends to rely too much on technical jargon in its promotions program. This finding would come from _____ .
   a) a situational analysis
   b) the marketing mix
   c) standardization and adaptation
   d) a GMIC analysis
(a; Moderate; p. 9)

50) Part of completing a successful _____ is preparing a marketing budget.
   a) situational analysis
   b) marketing plan
   c) marketing conceptualization
   d) adaptation of a marketing plan
(b; Moderate; p. 9)

51) Marketing tactics are _____.
   a) the day-by-day steps necessary to support marketing strategies
   b) an understanding of the environmentally-generated marketing problems
   c) all of the ingredients in a marketing mix, plus positioning and differentiation
   d) a form of marketing budget
(a; Moderate; p. 9)

52) Proctor and Gamble sets a goal to increase sales of Tide detergent to individuals between 20 and 25 years old in the next fiscal year. This is an example of _____ .
   a) a marketing mix
   b) a marketing objective
   c) a situational analysis
   d) evaluation of performance
(b; Moderate; p. 9)

53) The last stage of IMC development occurs when an organization _____ .
   a) identifies and coordinates all forms of external communications
   b) extends the scope of communication to include everyone in the organization
   c) puts technology at the forefront
   d) treats IMC as an investment and not a departmental function
(d; Moderate; pp. 12-13)

54) Bank of America has recently started analyzing the features customers use with ATM cards. This is an example of _____ .
   a) coordinating communication cross-functionally
   b) applying information technology
   c) a price and distribution system
   d) developing interpersonal communications
(b; Moderate; p. 16)

55) Hewlett-Packard's use of the phrase "we understand" is an example of _____ .
   a) marketing myopia
   b) franchise development
   c) an IMC umbrella designed to create a clear voice
   d) an effective marketing tactic due to the vagueness of the statement
(c, Moderate; p. 15)

56) Michael buys a CD player from the closest store because he doesn't think there is much of a difference between brands. This is an example of _____ .
   a) poor IMC communications
   b) standardization
   c) marketing integration
   d) brand parity
(d; Moderate; p. 18)

57) A company should make sure that all _____, including Web sites, phone lines, and advertisements present the same message and theme.
   a) contact points
   b) marketing plans
   c) account executives
   d) marketing objectives
   (a; Moderate; p. 18)

58) Which is <u>not</u> a cause of the decline in mass media advertising?
   a) satellite television offering more channels
   b) VCRs making it possible to "zap" commercials
   c) greater Internet use
   d) a greater number of new product introductions
   (d; Moderate; pp. 18-19)

59) Coca Cola runs the same advertisement in all French-speaking countries. This is an example of: _____ .
   a) a unified IMC theme
   b) standardization
   c) customization
   d) integration
   (b; Moderate; p. 20)

60) Buying on-line from Amazon.com rather than a record store is an example of _____ .
   a) a power shift to the consumer
   b) a power shift to the producer
   c) decline in the effectiveness of mass media
   d) a new form of wholesaling
   (a; Moderate; p. 16)

61) A creative's responsibilities include _____ .
   a) compiling databases regarding consumer behavior
   b) evaluation of the marketing plan
   c) developing advertisements and campaigns
   d) receiving the marketing messages from various sources
   (c; Challenging; p. 5)

62) An account executive's duties include _____ .
   a) preparing a database of consumer behavior
   b) strategic development of the marketing plan and ad campaign
   c) preparing the actual advertisements
   d) product development and application
   (b; Challenging; p. 4)

63) Which individual is most likely to work for the company that produces the product?
   a) an agency account executive
   b) a brand manager
   c) a media buyer
   d) a media planner
(b; Challenging; p. 5)

64) One of the more common trends in promotions is _____ .
   a) a decline in accountability
   b) an emphasis on print media
   c) a more integrated approach
   d) greater reliance on network advertising
(c; Challenging; p. 5)

65) When Susan comparison shops for an automobile, the most likely to be communications' senders are _____ .
   a) Honda and Toyota
   b) NBC and CSPAN
   c) The New York Times and the Chicago Sun Times
   d) The Internet and the Web
(a; Challenging; p. 5)

66) Which is encoding?
   a) a sales pitch recited by a salesperson
   b) database management finding a statistical oddity
   c) a chat room on the Internet
   d) a purchase decision
(a; Challenging; p. 5)

67) Which is clutter?
   a) watching six hours of television per day, the family average
   b) not paying attention to the only billboard within a 10-mile stretch of highway
   c) hearing a radio advertisement while reading one for a different company in a magazine
   d) a miscommunication between an ad agency and a brand manager
(c; Challenging; p. 8)

68) An example of a situational analysis is _____ .
   a) preparing an advertising budget
   b) developing a new TV advertisement
   c) discovering that consumers dislike the competitor's product design
   d) seeking to buy better advertising locations from a magazine
(c; Challenging; p. 9)

69) Predicting purchasing behavior of customers is more accurate today because of
_____.
   a) increased use of credit cards
   b) the UPC bar coding system and point-of-purchase systems
   c) the shift of power to retailers and consumers
   d) the ability of advertisers to accurately measure how many people watch or
      see advertisements
(b; Challenging; p. 16)

70) To combat brand parity, IBM might claim _____ .
   a) it is developing additional products
   b) it has found new customers to buy products
   c) it has new locations
   d) it sells better products
(d; Challenging; p. 18)

71) Which is not an example of a contact point?
   a) barnes&noble.com
   b) the white pages in a phone book
   c) a receptionist at Microsoft
   d) a sales clerk at a retail store
(b; Challenging; p. 18)

72) A survey by Roper Starch Worldwide found that only _____ percent of TV
viewers watch commercials during a television program.
   a) 3
   b) 19
   c) 30
   d) 50
(c; Challenging, p. 19)

73) An example of standardization is _____ .
   a) using the "Generation Next" theme in all of global Pepsi markets
   b) using women with their faces covered in ads for Islamic countries
   c) developing a Web site in several languages
   d) using the same salesperson to call on multiple countries
(a; Challenging; p. 20)

74) An example of adaptation is _____.
   a) Ford's One-World Ford Contour car
   b) not selling the McRib sandwich in Israel
   c) printing ads only in English for European countries
   d) using direct mail
(b; Challenging; p. 20)

75) In developing an IMC campaign, the two people who will work the closest together are the _____.
   a) account executive and creative
   b) account executive and brand manager
   c) creative and brand manager
   d) brand manager and global translator
(b; Challenging; p. 20)

76) In which of the following situations has noise disrupted the transmission of a message created by Reebok at the transmission device stage?
   a) the creative working on the assignment was working on several assignments at the same time and did a poor job of translating Reebok's desires into an ad
   b) the account executive was not clear about what Reebok wanted to accomplish with the ad
   c) the Reebok ad that was designed was in the middle of a sequence of television ads; as a result, few people watched or paid attention to it
   d) The person looking at the ad was also playing cards.
(c; Challenging, p. 6)

77) The Integrated Marketing Communications plan is a part of the _____ component of the marketing plan.
   a) situational analysis
   b) marketing objectives
   c) marketing strategies
   d) marketing tactics
(c; Challenging, p. 9)

78) A company has identified and coordinated all of the internal and external marketing communications to ensure that all speak with the same voice to all of their constituencies, both inside and outside of the company. The next step in ensuring that IMC is an organizational process is to _____.
   a) bring all of the company's brands and strategic business units under one umbrella
   b) include employees, distributors, retailers, dealers, and product package designers in all corporate communications
   c) treat IMC as an investment and not a departmental function
   d) bring technology to the forefront by applying information technology to their IMC program
(d; Challenging, p. 13)

79) The major force compelling firms to seek greater integration of advertising and marketing communications is _____.
a) developments in information technology
b) changes in channel power
c) increased global competition
d) decline in effectiveness of mass-media advertising
(a; Challenging, p. 14)

80) Within the marketing channel, manufacturers are having to invest more money in trade promotions because
a) consumers expect these promotions
b) retailers control what merchandise is on the store shelves
c) advertising is not enough to get consumers to purchase products
d) of the brand parity issue
(b; Challenging; p. 17)

Short-Answer Questions

81) Define IMC. What makes it different from traditional promotions programs?

IMC is the coordination and integration of all marketing communication tools, avenues, and sources within a company into a seamless program. IMC maximizes the impact on consumers and other end-users at minimal cost; it also affects all of the firm's business-to-business, customer-focused, and internally-oriented communications.

IMC is different because it is a more sweeping or strategic approach to marketing communications, designed to incorporate the entire company into the program.
(Moderate; pp. 8-9)

82) What are the components of the communications model?

The sender is the person(s) attempting to deliver a message or idea. Encoding is creating verbal and nonverbal cues that the sender uses to dispatch a message. A transmission device is any item that carries the message from the sender to the receiver. Decoding takes places when the receiver employs any set of his or her senses to capture the message. The receiver is the intended audience for a message.
(Moderate; pp. 5-8)

83)   What are the components of the marketing mix? The promotions mix?

The components of the marketing mix are: product, price, promotion, and distribution. The components of the promotions mix are: advertising, personal selling, sales promotions, direct marketing, and public relations.
(Easy; pp. 8-9)

84)   What are the steps in preparing a marketing plan?

The steps of preparation for a marketing plan are: 1) situational analysis; 2) establishing marketing objectives; 3) creating marketing budget; 4) devising the marketing strategy; 5) creating marketing tactics; and 6) marketing evaluation.
(Moderate; p. 9)

85)   The writers of this text describe an IMC plan as similar to a pyramid. Describe this approach.

The foundation is the IMC concept and:
- firm and brand image
     - understanding consumer buyer behaviors
     - understanding business-to-business buyer behaviors
     - promotions opportunity analysis
A second layer consisting of the advertising tools, including:
     - advertising management
     - advertising design: appeals
     - advertising design: executional frameworks
     - media selection
A third level containing other elements of the promotional mix, including:
     - trade promotions
     - consumer promotions
     - personal selling, database management, and customer relationship management
     - public relations and sponsorship programs
Integration tools, consisting of:
     - Internet marketing and e-commerce
     - IMC for small businesses and entrepreneurial ventures
     - evaluation
(Challenging; pp. 9-11)

86)   What recent trends make an IMC approach valuable to companies in the marketplace?

The development of information technology.
Changes in channel power.
Increases in global competition.
Maturing markets.

Integration of information by consumers.
Brand parity.
The decline in the effectiveness of mass media advertising.
(Challenging; pp. 14-19)

87) Describe the brand parity problem.

Brand parity is the problem that all products are basically equal in terms of the benefits they deliver.
(Easy; p. 18)

88) Describe contact points.

A contact point is any place in which the customer may interact with or acquire information about a firm. This would include advertising, service departments, personal selling situations, and phone calls or Internet inquiries to the company.
(Easy; p. 18)

89) Why is mass media advertising less effective?

Inventions, such as the VCR, make it possible to fast forward through commercials. Remotes can turn down the sound while commercials run. Cable offers more outlets and fewer viewers per outlet. All of the mass media, such as television, newspapers, radio, and magazines, suffer from a large number of ads, which creates clutter and makes it difficult for any one ad to standout and be noticed.
(Easy; pp. 18-19)

90) Define GMIC. What makes it so important in the twenty-first century marketplace?

GMIC is globally integrated marketing communications. It is important because many companies must compete in an international arena.
(Easy; p. 20)

CHAPTER 2
CORPORATE IMAGE AND BRAND MANAGEMENT

True-False Questions

1)   A corporate image contains both visible and intangible elements.
        (True; Easy; p. 29)

2)   Corporate image can provide psychological reinforcement and social acceptance of a purchasing decision.
        (True; Easy; p. 30)

3)   A strong corporate image does not affect the firm's ability to charge a higher price because it is so closely related to substantiation.
        (False; Easy; p. 31)

4)   Quality corporate logos are easily recognizable and elicit a consensual meaning among those in the target market.
        (True; Easy; p. 36)

5)   Brand equity is the perception that most products are relatively similar or have no distinct differences.
        (False; Easy; p. 39)

6)   A brand extension is the use of a new brand name to identify an old product.
        (False; Easy; p. 43)

7)   Positioning is the process of creating a perception in the consumer's mind regarding the nature of a company and its products relative to the competition.
        (True; Easy; p. 48)

8)   Perceptions of a corporate image are based solely on price and quality.
        (False; Moderate; p. 29)

9)   The notion that a logo can elicit a consensual meaning among customers is known as stimulus codability.
        (True; Moderate; p. 36)

10)   A family brand is a situation in which a series of companies produce one brand in a co-operative venture.
        (False; Moderate; p. 37)

11)   Domination is a negative force in brand equity because it suggests poor publicity has affected the brand.
        (False; Moderate; p. 40)

12) Ingredient branding is the placement of one brand within another, such as NutraSweet as part of Diet Coke.
(True; Moderate; p. 44)

13) Private brands and private label programs diminished greatly in the 1990s, due to increasing levels of consumer affluence.
(False; Moderate; p. 45)

14) Using an attribute positioning strategy would involve emphasizing a particular trait or characteristic of the product.
(True; Moderate; p. 48)

15) Brand equity is a good weapon against consumers switching to another brand due to sales promotions.
(True; Challenging; p. 40)

16) Rejuvenating an image is related more to raising prices than to finding new customers or selling new products.
(False; Challenging; p. 34)

17) Nike has spent considerable resources developing stimulus codability related to its "Swoosh."
(True; Challenging; p. 36)

18) Oreo milkshakes sold in a Dairy Question is an example of complementary branding.
(True; Challenging; p. 45)

19) A product user positioning strategy is creating a new or unusual product class that the brand can dominate.
(False; Challenging; p. 49)

20) In positioning products, it is important to be sure that the positioning strategy chosen is relevant to consumers and provides them with a benefit the consumer considers useful in decision making.
(True; Challenging; p. 51)

Multiple-Choice Questions

21) The Dell Dude is an example of _____ .
   a) an advertising success based on building greater brand awareness
   b) an advertising program based on stimulus codability
   c) the importance of a quality tagline
   d) an advertising failure because the Dude was more recognizable than the product
(a; Easy, pp. 26-27)

22) Corporate image is important to consumers for every reason below <u>except</u> _____ .
    a) reassurance regarding purchase decisions of familiar products in new settings
    b) a method of expanding a purchase choice by identifying new alternatives
    c) reduction of search time in purchase decisions
    d) assurance concerning purchases where there is little previous experience
(b; Easy; p. 30)

23) Corporate image is important to vendors for every reason below <u>except</u> _____ .
    a) allows retailers to control the channel
    b) positive word-of-mouth endorsements
    c) the ability to attract quality employees
    d) the ability to charge a higher price or fee
(a; Easy; p. 31)

24) Changing an image is most necessary _____ .
    a) every few years
    b) when the company is ready for a change
    c) when target markets shrink or disappear
    d) when a competitor enters the market
(c; Easy; p. 35)

25) Logos help with in-store shopping because _____ .
    a) consumers make decisions in the store
    b) logos move traffic past goods which are not being purchased
    c) they are a form of clutter
    d) consumers have made up their minds prior to arrival
(a; Easy; p. 36)

26) A family brand is _____ .
    a) one in which a company offers a series or group of products under one brand name
    b) a type of extension or flanker brand
    c) a logo or theme
    d) a brand for a substitute good
(a; Easy; p. 37)

27) Which is <u>not</u> true concerning brand equity?
    a) it allows the company to charge a higher price
    b) it reduces differentiation
    c) it is helpful in business-to-business markets
    d) it is helpful in international markets
(b; Easy; p. 40)

28) Brand equity includes all of the following <u>except</u> _____ .
    a) brand name recognition
    b) brand name recall
    c) domination
    d) exaggeration
(d; Easy; p. 40)

29) Which is a brand extension?
    a) the use of a family brand
    b) creation of a logo which further explains the brand
    c) design of a public relations campaign to support a brand
    d) using an established brand name on goods or services not related to the core brand
(d; Easy; p. 43)

30) Which is ingredient branding?
    a) placing one brand within another
    b) placing a promotional item in a package
    c) a joint venture of two brands in one product
    d) marketing two brands together to encourage co-consumption
(a; Easy p. 44)

31) Which is cooperative branding?
    a) private labeling with a major brand
    b) placing one brand in another as a form of cooperation
    c) the joint venture of two or more brands in one product
    d) marketing two brands together to encourage co-consumption
(c; Easy; p. 44)

32) Which is complementary branding?
    a) using a private label to complement the main brand
    b) placing one brand within another brand
    c) the joint venture of two or more brands in one product
    d) marketing two brands together to encourage co-consumption
(d; Easy; p. 45)

33) One reason private labels have been successful is _____ .
    a) they are manufactured by generic manufacturing firms
    b) because they do not have to spend any money on advertising
    c) loyalty towards stores is rising while loyalty toward brands is declining
    d) they are sold only in discount stores
(c; Easy; p. 46)

34) A package does all of the following, except _____ .
    a) create an extension brand when the label is modified
    b) contribute to the overall marketing program
    c) protect the contents
    d) help make the product identifiable, even when the label is missing
(a; Easy; p. 38)

35) Which is positioning?
    a) a form of logo
    b) a form of extension brand
    c) creating a perception in the consumer's mind regarding the nature of a brand relative to the competition
    d) creating the impression that the company is from a particular industry
(c; Easy; p. 48)

36) In promoting a desired corporate or brand image, the most difficult would be to _____ .
    a) create a new image for a new product
    b) reinforce a current image that is consistent with consumers' views
    c) rejuvenate a current image that is consistent with consumers' views
    d) modify a current image because it is not consistent with what the company wants to project
(d; Moderate; p. 32)

37) Distinguishing a product from its competitors based on who uses it is a positioning strategy based on _____ .
    a) product user
    b) product class
    c) use or application
    d) competitors
(a; Easy; p. 49)

38) Creating a perception in the consumer's mind regarding the nature of a company and its products relative to the competition is called _____ .
    a) positioning
    b) brand management
    c) stimulus codability
    d) corporate image
(a; Easy; p. 48)

39) All of the following are tangible components of a corporate image except _____ .
    a) goods and services sold
    b) retail outlets where the product is sold
    c) advertising, promotions, and other forms of communication
    d) ideals and beliefs of corporate personnel
(d; Easy; p. 29)

40) In the mind of the consumer, a strong corporate image is linked to _____ .
   a) perceptions of economic conditions
   b) more positive ratings by financial advisors
   c) reduction of search time in purchase decisions
   d) a higher price
   (c; Moderate; p. 30)

41) From the perspective of the corporation, a strong brand image is related to all the following except _____ .
   a) being able to charge a higher price
   b) psychological reinforcement and social acceptance
   c) more frequent purchases by customers
   d) more favorable ratings by financial observers
   (b; Moderate; p. 31)

42) Radio Shack's attempt to demystify technology to consumers using the new slogan, "You've got questions, we've got answers," is a form of _____ .
   a) brand equity
   b) stimulus codability
   c) brand parity
   d) image rejuvenation
   (d; Moderate; p. 34)

43) Stimulus codability is _____ .
   a) a form of brand name
   b) the perception that the brand is known
   c) consensually held meanings among customers
   d) another name for product positioning
   (c; Moderate; p. 36)

44) When Black and Decker introduced a new form of wrench with the name "Black and Decker Adjustable Wrench," the name was a _____ .
   a) family brand
   b) cooperative brand
   c) flanker brand
   d) complementary brand
   (a; Moderate; p. 37)

45) When a customer believes Black and Decker makes the best and most reliable tools, this is an example of _____ .
   a) brand parity
   b) brand equity
   c) brand cooperation
   d) brand decision
   (b; Moderate; p. 39)

46) If consumers believe that Crest is the number one toothpaste for fighting cavities, this is an example of _____ .
   a) corporate image
   b) brand domination
   c) brand recognition
   d) brand evaluation
   (b; Moderate; p. 40)

47) When Proctor and Gamble adds a new laundry detergent called "Reach" to its current line of laundry detergents, Reach is considered a _____ .
   a) brand extension
   b) brand fabrication
   c) flanker brand
   d) complementary brand
   (c; Moderate; p. 43)

48) An Intel Pentium IV processor placed inside computers is a form of _____ .
   a) ingredient branding
   b) flanker brand
   c) cooperative branding
   d) complementary branding
   (a; Moderate; p. 44)

49) Selling Reese's Peanut Butter Cup milkshakes at the DQ is an example of _____ .
   a) flanker branding
   b) extension branding
   c) cooperative branding
   d) complementary branding
   (d; Moderate; p. 45)

50) Which is not true concerning private labels?
   a) quality levels of many private label products have improved
   b) prices for private labels are going up in many markets
   c) consumers still perceive private labels to be inferior to manufacturer's brands
   d) some firms have begun advertising private labels
   (c; Moderate; p. 46)

51) The Nike Swoosh is an example of a _____ .
   a) brand
   b) package
   c) label
   d) logo
   (c; Moderate; p. 39)

52) Positioning a product using the attribute strategy would involve promoting _____ .
   a) a product trait or characteristic which sets the product apart from its competitors
   b) the product in relation to the competition
   c) an extension of a brand name
   d) the price of the product in relation to its best attribute
(a; Moderate; p. 49)

53) Use or application positioning involves promoting _____ .
   a) a product trait or characteristic which sets the product apart from its competitors
   b) a product relative to the competition
   c) the type of individuals or businesses that use the product
   d) creating a memorable set of uses for a product
(d; Moderate; p. 49)

54) Using the Playboy bunny logo in a positioning strategy is an example of positioning by _____ .
   a) attribute
   b) use or application
   c) product user
   d) a cultural symbol
(d; Moderate, p. 49)

55) In developing a strong brand name, all of these are good questions to ask except _____ .
   a) how long has the brand name been in existence?
   b) what are the most compelling benefits?
   c) what one word best describes the brand?
   d) what is important to consumers when purchasing the product?
(a; Moderate, p. 37)

56) New trends in packaging include all of the following except _____ .
   a) protect the product from tampering
   b) meet consumer needs for speed, convenience, and portability
   c) contemporary and striking design
   d) designed for ease of use
(a; Moderate; pp. 38-39)

57) Successful brand development includes all of the following except _____ .
   a) continuing commitment to the brand
   b) understanding the market the brand reaches
   c) using brand metrics to evaluate the value of the brand
   d) leveraging the effects of brand penetration
(c; Moderate; p. 41)

58) Co-branding can take all of the following forms except _____ .
   a) flanker brand
   b) ingredient brand
   c) cooperative brand
   d) complementary brand
   (a; Moderate; p. 44)

59) In terms of brand management, the best approach for coping with a recession _____ .
   a) is to offer private brands
   b) depends on a brand's product category, unique selling points and position in the market place
   c) is to enhance the brand's equity
   d) reduce the price of the product
   (b; Moderate; p. 47)

60) If a company feels that offering a new product under the current brand name may adversely affect the current brand, the best strategy would be to introduce the product as a(n) _____ .
   a) brand extension
   b) ingredient brand
   c) flanker brand
   d) co-brand
   (c; Challenging; p. 43)

61) Which is an intangible element of a corporate image?
   a) the corporate name and logo
   b) a sense of security in buying the product
   c) the employees
   d) a package and label
   (b; Challenging; p. 29)

62) McDonald's use of a "dollar menu" in 2002 illustrates the attempt to _____ .
   a) establish a new corporate image
   b) rejuvenate a corporate image
   c) create a corporate image
   d) build brand equity with former customers
   (b; Challenging; p. 34)

63) Corporate logos _____ .
   a) are unrelated to image but are related to positioning
   b) help with recall of ads and brands
   c) usually are inexpensive to develop
   d) increase search time in product purchase decisions
   (b; Challenging; p. 36)

64) Quality logos and corporate names should meet all of the following tests <u>except</u> _____ .
   a) be easy to pronounce
   b) be familiar
   c) elicit a consensual meaning among those in the firm's target market
   d) evoke positive feelings
(a; Challenging; p. 36)

65) Which is true concerning brand name recognition and brand equity?
   a) they are unrelated
   b) they are synonymous
   c) equity is more difficult to establish than recognition
   d) recognition is more difficult to establish than equity
(c; Challenging; p. 40)

66) Shoebox Greetings is Hallmark's _____ .
   a) flanker brand
   b) complementary brand
   c) cooperative brand
   d) ingredient brand
(a; Challenging ; p. 43)

67) A Pillsbury cake mix featuring Hershey's Chocolate is a form of _____ .
   a) flanker brand
   b) cooperative brand
   c) ingredient brand
   d) complementary brand
(c; Challenging; p. 44)

68) American Express Traveler's Cheques are a form of _____ .
   a) flanker brand
   b) brand extension
   c) cooperative brand
   d) complementary brand
(b; Challenging; p. 43)

69) Which of the following is most likely to be affected by a recession?
   a) luxury goods
   b) necessities
   c) flanker brand and extensions
   d) cooperative brands
(a; Challenging; p. 47)

70) Which has the smallest effect on a product's positioning strategy?
   a) price/quality relationship
   b) economic conditions
   c) competitive activities
   d) consumer beliefs
(b; Challenging; pp. 48-51)

71) Arby's assessment that 40% of households in neighborhoods within one mile of a unit purchased a roast beef sandwich from the company in the past year reflects _____ .
   a) Arby's market position
   b) the level of Arby's market penetration
   c) Arby's market inclusion
   d) Arby's logo recognition by local consumers
(b; Challenging; p. 41)

72) Ford's statement that company advertising has resulted in increased awareness of the Focus, greater recall and recognition of the brand, and consequently increased consumer willingness to buy the car is based on _____ .
   a) market position
   b) market penetration
   c) brand metrics
   d) brand dynamics
(c; Challenging, p. 42)

73) When V8 Vegetable Soup is promoted as having less sodium for individuals on a low-sodium diet, they are using a positioning strategy based on _____ .
   a) attributes
   b) use or application
   c) product user
   d) product class
(c; Challenging; pp. 48-49)

74) Co-brand succeeds the best when _____ .
   a) the two brands are unrelated
   b) a well-known brand is attached to a lesser-known brand
   c) a private label is co-branded with a manufacturer's brand
   d) it builds the brand equity of both brands
(d; Challenging; p. 45)

75) An advertisement by State Farm informing consumers about the company's goal of making driving safer is an example of an ad designed to _____ .
   a) rejuvenate State Farm's image
   b) enhance State Farm's corporate image
   c)   reposition State Farm based on the product attribute of safety
   d) build a stronger family brand
(b; Challenging; p. 29)

76) General Mills was successful in introducing a new flavor of Pillsbury homemade-style biscuits because _____ .
    a) of a strong family brand
    b) of General Mills' current positioning strategy
    c) of their Pillsbury private brand label
    d) of the Pillsbury package design
(a; Challenging; p. 31)

77) A particular brand is salient for consumers under all of the following situations <u>except</u> when they_____ .
    a) are aware of the brand
    b) regard the product and brand as a good value
    c) recommend it to others
    d) position it against the market leader
(d; Challenging; pp. 36-37)

78) To build brand equity, the amount of the communication budget that should be spent on techniques such as coupons, sweepstakes, premiums, price-offs, etc. to drive sales should not exceed _____ .
    a) 50%
    b) 40%
    c) 30%
    d) 20%
(c; Challenging; p. 40)

79) Leveraging the effects of market penetration means a brand should build effective expansion programs and _____ .
    a) position their product using the competitor strategy
    b) rejuvenate their brand image
    c) fend off any attacks by competitors
    d) develop a strong brand logo
(c; Challenging; pp. 41)

80) Which of the following statements about image is false?
    a) Reinforcing or rejuvenating a current image that is consistent with the view of consumers is easier to accomplish than changing a well-established image.
    b) It is relatively easy to change the images people hold about a given company.
    c) Any negative or bad press can quickly destroy an image that took years to build.
    d) The image being projected must accurately portray the firm and coincide with its goods and services.
(b, Challenging, p. 32)

Short-Answer Questions

81)   What functions are related to corporate image from a consumer's perspective?

1. Assurance regarding purchase decisions of familiar products in unfamiliar settings
2. Assurance concerning purchases where there is little previous experience
3. Reduction of search time in purchase decisions
4. Psychological reinforcement and social acceptance of purchase decisions

(Moderate, p. 30)

82)   What four tests should quality logos and corporate names pass?

1. They should be easily recognizable.
2. They should be familiar.
3. They should elicit a consensual meaning among those in the firm's target market.
4. They should evoke positive feelings.

(Moderate, p. 36)

83)   What three forms of co-branding are there? Define each one.

1. Ingredient branding is placement of one brand within another brand.
2. Cooperative branding is the joint venture of two brands or more into a new product or service.
3. Complementary branding is marketing of two brands together to encourage co-consumptions or co-purchases.

(Moderate, pp. 44-45)

84)   What are the types of product positioning?

1. Attributes
2. Competitors
3. Use or application
4. Price/quality relationship
5. Product user
6. Product class
7. Cultural symbol positioning

(Moderate, pp. 48-49)

85) What are the benefits of a strong corporate image in the eyes of the company?

1. Extension of positive consumer feelings to new products
2. The ability to charge a higher price or fee
3. Consumer loyalty leading to more frequent purchases
4. Positive word-of-mouth endorsements
5. The ability to attract quality employees
6. More favorable ratings by financial observers and analysts

(Challenging, p. 31)

86) Why have private brands or private labels been more successful in recent years?

1. Quality levels have improved
2. Higher prices can be charged
3. Loyalty toward stores is higher than loyalty to brands
4. Increased advertising of private labels

(Challenging, pp. 45-46)

87) When should a company consider rejuvenating its image and how should it be done?

A company should consider rejuvenating its image when sales have declined or a competitor has taken a strong market position in the industry. Any time the brand has suffered a decline in brand equity is a good time to consider rejuvenating an image. Rejuvenating an image requires developing a campaign that is consistent with the current image while at the same time incorporating new elements into the image to expand the firm's target market and to reconnect with previous customers.

(Challenging, pp. 34)

88) When developing a strong brand name, what are some typical questions that should be asked?

1. What are the most compelling benefits?
2. What emotions are elicited by the brand either during or after the purchase?
3. What one word best describes the brand?
4. What is important to consumers in the purchase of the product?

(Challenging, p. 37)

89) What are the traditional elements that have to be incorporated into packaging design and what are the new trends that impact packaging?

Traditional elements of packaging include:
1. Protect the product inside
2. Provide for ease in shipping, moving, and handling
3. Provide for easy placement on store shelves
4. Prevent or reduce the possibility of theft
5. Prevent tampering

New trends in packaging include:
1. Meet consumer needs for speed, convenience, and portability
2. Must be contemporary and striking
3. Must be designed for ease of use
(Challenging, pp. 38-39)

90) Identify the steps in building a high level of brand equity.

1. Research and analyze what it would take to make the brand distinctive.
2. Decide what makes the brand unique.
3. Boldly communicate the unique selling point of the brand.
4. Spend no more than 30% of the communication budget on driving sales, which includes sales promotions, such as coupons, premiums, contests, etc.
5. Make domination the goal.
6. Deliver on the promise or uniqueness being communicated.
(Challenging, p. 40)

CHAPTER 3
CONSUMER BUYER BEHAVIOR

True-False Questions

1)   The first step of the consumer buying decision-making process is identification of alternatives.
        (False; Easy p. 61)

2)   An internal search for purchasing alternatives and information may begin with dissatisfaction with the last purchase.
        (True; Easy; p. 62)

3)   The cognitive component of an attitude is a person's mental image, understanding, and interpretation of the product.
        (True; Easy; p. 65)

4)   Values are loosely held attitudes about various topics or concepts.
        (False; Easy; p. 66)

5)   The central route of the Elaboration Likelihood Model processes peripheral cues.
        (False; Easy; p. 67)

6)   The inept set in a series of choices is the set of brands that are not considered because they elicit negative feelings.
        (True; Easy; p. 72)

7)   Post-purchase cognitive dissonance is most likely to appear following an impulse buy of a low-priced item.
        (False; Easy; p. 75)

8)   The evoked set in a purchase decision consists of brands that have been purchased previously.
        (False; Moderate; p. 62)

9)   The motivation to search for purchase alternatives is largely determined by the individual's age and status.
        (False; Moderate; pp. 62-64)

10)   The conative component of an attitude is the part most directly connected to taking action.
        (True; Moderate; p. 65)

11) Music, actors, and background are processed through the peripheral route of the Elaboration Likelihood Model.
    (True; Moderate; p. 68)

12) The Hedonic, Experiential Model focuses on rational processes.
    (False; Moderate; p. 68)

13) A cognitive map explains search motives using ability, time, and how much the individual likes shopping.
    (False; Moderate; p. 69)

14) Divorcees or second-chancers usually have low household incomes and are between the ages of 40 and 59.
    (False; Moderate; p. 77)

15) A person considering only Coke, Pepsi, and Royal Crown Cola at a vending machine is employing his or her evoked set.
    (True; Challenging; p. 72)

16) The need for cognition is a personality characteristic that links the drive to consider alternatives with the drive to take action quickly.
    (False; Challenging; p. 63)

17) Cognitive maps can be altered to incorporate situations in which a message or idea has no current linkages within a person's levels and layers of thinking.
    (True; Challenging; pp. 70-71)

18) It costs five to six times more to retain a customer than develop a new customer.
    (False; Challenging; p. 75)

19) Utility may be derived from post-purchase cognitive dissonance in which a person gains a greater sense of control.
    (False; Challenging; pp. 75, 79)

20) One recent trend in purchasing decisions is a greater emphasis on indulgences and pleasure binges, even after the events of September 11, 2001.
    (True; Challenging; p. 81)

Multiple-Choice Questions

21) In which stage of a buying decision would a person recall his or her evoked set?
   a) problem recognition
   b) information search
   c) actual purchase
   d) post-purchase evaluation

   (b; Easy; p. 62)

22) Which factor does <u>not</u> have a direct impact on the amount of time a person would be willing to spend on an external search of purchase alternatives?
   a) ability
   b) motivation
   c) costs
   d) day of the week

   (d; Easy; p. 63)

23) Which is enduring involvement in a purchase decision?
   a) a purchase situation that is always important to a consumer
   b) a purchase situation that is sometimes important to a consumer
   c) purchase of a luxury item
   d) purchase of a necessity product

   (a; Easy; p. 63)

24) Which is the most action-oriented component of an attitude?
   a) affective
   b) cognitive
   c) conative
   d) expressive

   (c; Easy; p. 65)

25) Which is the most emotional component of an attitude?
   a) affective
   b) cognitive
   c) conative
   d) rational

   (a; Easy; p. 65)

26) Which is the most rational component of an attitude?
   a) affective
   b) cognitive
   c) conative
   d) behavioral

   (b; Easy; p. 65)

27) The Elaboration Likelihood Model's central processing route is the most _____ .
   a) rational
   b) emotional
   c) behavioral
   d) expressive
   (a; Easy; p. 67)

28) The Elaboration Likelihood Model's peripheral route more carefully considers _____ .
   a) major message arguments
   b) core themes
   c) embedded cues
   d) calls to action
   (c; Easy; p. 68)

29) The driving force behind a purchase decision using the HEM is _____ .
   a) seeking pleasure
   b) being rational
   c) investigating all alternatives
   d) not acting impulsively
   (a; Easy; p. 68)

30) In the HEM or hedonic, experiential model, the key element of an ad is _____ .
   a) the time of day it is shown
   b) the use of music and emotion
   c) the use of logic and reasoning
   d) the gender of the consumer
   (b; Easy; p. 68)

31) Which is a simulation of the knowledge structures embedded in an individual's brain?
   a) the Elaboration Likelihood Model
   b) the Hedonic, Experiential Model
   c) a cognitive map
   d) the components of attitudes
   (c; Easy; p. 69)

32) Which is not part of a cognitive map?
   a) levels
   b) layers
   c) linkages
   d) behaviors
   (d; Easy; p. 70)

33) Which is a set of brands a consumer knows about but has neither positive nor negative feelings?
   a) inept set
   b) inert set
   c) cognitive set
   d) conative set
(b; Easy; p. 72)

34) Which is a set of brands a person will <u>not</u> consider due to negative feelings?
   a) inept set
   b) inert set
   c) negative set
   d) alternative set
(a; Easy; p. 72)

35) Using the multi-attribute approach, an individual considers _____ .
   a) beliefs about attributes and the importance of those attributes
   b) layers, levels, and linkages toward the product
   c) cognitive, conative, and affective reactions to the product
   d) the central and peripheral route of reasoning
(a; Easy; p. 72)

36) Using the affect referral approach to decision-making, the person considers _____ .
   a) attributes and the importance of attributes
   b) the brand he or she likes the best
   c) cognitive and conative cues
   d) central and peripheral cues
(b; Easy; p. 72)

37) A final purchasing decision may change due to all of the following <u>except</u> _____ .
   a) a desire for variety
   b) an impulse decision
   c) the influence of friends or families
   d) a lower price for a brand in the consumer's inept set
(d; Easy; pp. 72-73)

38) Which is <u>not</u> a traditional factor that affects purchase decisions?
   a) heredity
   b) home environment
   c) family life cycles
   d) clanning
(d; Moderate; pp. 76, 81)

39) Which is not a new trend that affects purchase decisions?
   a) changing attitudes and values
   b) time pressure
   c) political trends
   d) indulgences and pleasure binges
(c; Moderate; p. 80)

40) Repetition is _____ for individuals processing information using the peripheral route of the ELM than if the individual processes the information using the central processing route.
   a) less important
   b) more important
   c) of equal importance
   d) not a factor
(b; Moderate; pp. 67-68)

41) When a person conducts an internal search and finds an acceptable choice among his or her evoked set, what would be the next step?
   a) search for additional information
   b) the purchase
   c) evaluation of the alternatives
   d) problem identification
(b; Moderate; pp. 62, 73)

42) An evoked set does not contain _____ .
   a) brands a person considers
   b) brands where a positive experience took place
   c) brands which have been previously purchased
   d) brands the consumer knows little about
(d; Moderate; p. 62)

43) Which does not affect the individual's ability to conduct an external search for additional information?
   a) educational level
   b) specific knowledge of product category
   c) level of emotion
   d) knowledge of brands being offered
(c; Moderate; p. 63)

44) Which is not a part of the degree of involvement in a purchase decision?
   a) whether or not it is relevant to the consumer's existing needs and wants
   b) whether or not the consumer has sufficient intelligence and education
   c) whether or not the purchase is always important to the consumer
   d) whether or not situational involvement is present
(b; Moderate; p. 63)

45) Perceived costs of a purchase decision do not include _____ .
   a) the actual price or cost
   b) the subjective costs associated with the search
   c) the economic conditions of the area
   d) the opportunity costs of foregoing other activities to make the search
   (c; Moderate; p. 64)

46) An impulse buy probably means the consumer acted on which component of an attitude?
   a) affective
   b) cognitive
   c) conative
   d) enthusiasm
   (c; Moderate; p. 66)

47) A low price, low involvement purchase is likely to begin with which component of an attitude?
   a) affective
   b) cognitive
   c) conative
   d) remorse
   (c; Moderate; p. 66)

48) If an ad appeals to a person's emotions first, the ad is using a(n) _____ .
   a) affective approach
   b) cognitive approach
   c) conative approach
   d) multi-cultural approach
   (a; Moderate; p. 66)

49) If an ad appeals to a person's emotions first, the ad is likely to be based on _____ .
   a) the central route of the ELM for information processing
   b) the HEM model of information processing
   c) a cognitive map
   d) the multi-attribute approach method of evaluating alternatives
   (b; Moderate; p. 68)

50) Which most closely matches the central route of the Elaboration Likelihood Model?
   a) affective component of attitude
   b) cognitive component of attitude
   c) conative component of attitude
   d) attribute component of attitude
   (b; Moderate; p. 67)

51) The peripheral route of the Elaboration Likelihood model matches the _____ .
   a) affective component of attitude
   b) cognitive component of attitude
   c) conative component of attitude
   d) attribute component of attitude
   (a; Moderate; p. 68)

52) The primary assumption of the HEM is that consumers _____ .
   a) make irrational purchase decisions based on feelings and emotions
   b) make rational decisions
   c) purchase products that fit their family budget
   d) consider all of the alternatives before making a purchase
   (a; Moderate; p. 68)

53) Where are layers and levels of cognition found?
   a) cognitive maps
   b) maps of attitudes
   c) Elaboration Likelihood Models
   d) Hedonic, Experiential Models
   (a; Moderate; p. 69)

54) A person buys a Honda Accord without considering other brands. Which model best explains this decision?
   a) cognitive map
   b) evoked set
   c) multi-attribute
   d) affect referral
   (d; Moderate; p. 72)

55) A person carefully considers price, sound quality, and space taken by a new stereo, and sound quality is the most important. Which model explains this thinking?
   a) cognitive map
   b) evoked set
   c) multi-attribute
   d) affect referral
   (c; Moderate; p. 72)

56) Which does not explain a shift from the chosen alternative to another brand while at the store?
   a) cognitive map
   b) the desire for variety
   c) an impulse purchase
   d) the influence of a friend or relative
   (a; Moderate, p. 73)

57) Post-purchase cognitive dissonance is most likely in _____ .
   a) low involvement purchases
   b) high involvement purchases
   c) purchases of low-cost items
   d) a purchase made out of habit
   (b; Moderate; p. 75)

58) First families are those with _____ .
   a) high levels of credit
   b) low rates of credit debt
   c) children that have not yet reached the teenage years
   d) a single parent head of household
   (c; Moderate; p. 78)

59) The conscious decision to stay home more, entertain friends, and focus on family following the September 11 tragedy reflects which trend?
   a) evolving demographics
   b) heredity and home environment
   c) new family life cycles
   d) the impact of life-changing events
   (d; Moderate; p. 77)

60) Pleasure cruises and exotic vacations take advantage of which trend?
   a) cocooning
   b) life-changing events
   c) heredity and home environment
   d) indulgences and pleasure binges
   (d; Moderate; p. 81)

61) Which is not part of the motivation to search externally for a purchase option?
   a) specific product knowledge
   b) enduring involvement
   c) cognitive consistency
   d) costs and benefits
   (c; Challenging; p. 63)

62) A person who reasons that a Kenmore refrigerator has the best price/quality relationship has been using _____ .
   a) affective component of attitude formation
   b) cognitive component of attitude formation
   c) conative component of attitude formation
   d) experiential component of attitude formation
   (b; Challenging; p. 65)

63) A person who is swayed by an ad that incites fear is using the _____ component of attitude.
  a) affective
  b) cognitive
  c) conative
  d) short-term memory
(a; Challenging; p. 66)

64) A consumer who dislikes the spokesperson in a television will likely use which information processing method and route?
  a) central route of the Elaboration Likelihood model
  b) peripheral route of the Elaboration Likelihood model
  c) central route of the hedonic, experiential model
  d) peripheral route of the hedonic, experiential model
(b; Challenging; pp. 67-69)

65) Which method of information processing is most likely to result in a person ignoring long-term consequences of behaviors while giving in to short-term pleasures?
  a) ELM
  b) HEM
  c) affective referral
  d) multi-attribute model
(b; Challenging; p. 68)

66) Feelings of fun, excitement, and experiencing the unusual uses which approach to create advertisements?
  a) central route of the Elaboration Likelihood Model
  b) the Hedonic, Experiential Model
  c) current linkages in a cognitive map
  d) expressive components of a multi-attribute approach
(b; Challenging; p. 68)

67) A logic driven business-to-business ad focuses on _____ .
  a) central route of the Elaboration Likelihood Model
  b) peripheral route of the Elaboration Likelihood Model
  c) experiential route of the Hedonic, Experiential Model
  d) middle levels of a cognitive map
(a; Challenging; pp. 67-69)

68) The choice to buy a cup of Starbuck's latte costing over $3.00 is probably driven by which model?
  a) central route of the ELM
  b) peripheral route of the ELM
  c) central route of the HEM
  d) peripheral route of the HEM
(d; Challenging; pp. 68-69)

69)   When an individual considers all the ideas that come to mind when the name of a product is mentioned, which best explains the thinking?
        a) the Elaboration Likelihood Model
        b) the Hedonic, Experiential Model
        c) a cognitive map
        d) affect referral
(c; Challenging; p. 69)

70)   A consumer thinks about buying lunch and quickly eliminates Long John Silver's because he got sick the last time he ate there. Which explains the process?
        a) the central route of the Elaboration Likelihood model
        b) a new, lower rating in the person's multi-attribute evaluation
        c) Long John Silver's being in the person's inept set
        d) being moved by a negative affect referral
(c; Challenging; p. 72)

71)   A consumer thinks about buying lunch and quickly decides to go to Long John Silver's because they have his favorite shrimp. Which explains the choice?
        a) multi-attribute reasoning
        b) the inert set
        c) a high degree of involvement
        d) affect referral
(d; Challenging; p. 72)

72)   A teenager taking forever to buy a pair of jeans because of all the factors involved, price, color, social status, style is probably using which approach?
        a) Hedonic, Experiential model
        b) inept and inert sets
        c) a multi-attribute approach
        d) affect referral
(c; Challenging; p. 72)

73)   A person always drinks Coke but decides on Royal Crown Cola at the store instead. Which process explains this choice?
        a) desire for variety
        b) hedonism
        c) affect referral
        d) new inert set
(a; Challenging; p. 73)

74) Spending money you don't have on a designer outfit is part of which trend in buying decision-making?
  a) indulgence and pleasure binge
  b) affect referral
  c) reconfigured cognitive map
  d) being a second-chancer
(a; Challenging; p. 81)

75) In purchasing clothes, which of the following would have the greatest impact on the purchase decision?
  a) social acceptance
  b) situational factors
  c) time pressure
  d) home environment
(a; Challenging; p. 78)

76) Which of the following is not a change in cultural values and attitudes that has impacted consumer buyer behavior?
  a) sexual orientation
  b) tolerance of nudity
  c) decline in the divorce rate
  d) racial tolerance and acceptance of diversity in society
(c; Challenging; p. 80)

77) For most consumers, going to the Rainforest Café to eat would be an example of a purchase to satisfy _____ .
  a) psychological needs
  b) epistemic needs
  c) emotional needs
  d) social needs
(b; Challenging; p. 79)

78) Which is not evidence of cocooning?
  a) buying an elaborate home
  b) a gourmet kitchen area
  c) taking a pleasure cruise
  d) moving to a gated theme community
(c; Challenging; p. 81)

79) In terms of cognitive mapping, if most consumers have not considered Sunkist oranges as a substitute for salt, then an advertisement that conveys such a message to consumers would be attempting to _____ .
   a) strengthen a linkage that already exists
   b) modifying a current linkage
   c) create a new linkage
   d) create a new layer
(c; Challenging; pp. 70-71)

80) Which attitude development sequence is being used if an advertisement by Pampers highlights a parent's love for their baby?
   a) cognitive -> affective -> conative
   b) affective -> conative -> cognitive
   c) conative -> cognitive -> affective
   d) cognitive -> conative -> affective
(b; Challenging; pp. 65-66)

Short-Answer Questions

81) Name the steps of the consumer buying decision-making process.

   1. problem recognition
   2. information search
   3. evaluation of alternatives
   4. purchase decision
   5. post-purchase evaluation
(Easy, p. 61)

82) The amount of time a consumer spends on an external information search depends on four factors. What are they?

   1. ability
   2. motivation
   3. costs
   4. benefits
(Moderate, p. 63)

83) A consumer's level of motivation in making an external search depends on three factors. What are they?

   1. level of involvement
   2. need for cognition
   3. level of shopping enthusiasm
(Moderate, p. 63)

84)   An attitude consists of three components. Name and describe each one.

1) The affective component is the feelings or emotions a person holds regarding a topic, object, or idea. 2) The cognitive component is the person's mental images, understanding, and interpretations of the person, object, or idea. 3) The conative component is an individual's intentions, actions, or behavior.
(Moderate, p. 65)

85)   What are the two pathways in the Elaboration Likelihood Model? Describe each.

1) The central route occurs when the consumer cognitively processes a message giving a high degree of attention to the major or core elements of the message. 2) The peripheral route is followed when the individual pays attention to other, more marginal cues imbedded in a communication message, such as actors, music, and background.
(Moderate, pp. 67-68)

86)   Cognitive maps consist of three elements. What are they?

1) The layers and levels, which link thoughts and ideas together regarding a subject or product. 2) The factors, which affect linkages that already exist, such as advertisements or direct marketing pieces. 3) The situations in which a message has no linkage so that one must be created.
(Moderate, p. 70)

87)   An evoked set contains purchase alternatives. What are the other two elements?

1) The inept set, which consists of brands that will not be considered because they elicit negative feelings. 2) The inert set, which holds the brands the consumer is aware of but has neither negative nor positive feelings about those products.
(Moderate, p. 72)

88)   A consumer has made a mental choice, but buys a different alternative after reaching the store. What factors can explain the shift?

1. a temporary change in the consumer's situation
2. a desire for variety
3. an impulse purchase
4. an ad, promotion or marketing material at the store
5. the influence of a friend or relative
(Challenging, p. 73)

89) What traditional factors affect purchase decisions?

1. Demographics
2. Heredity and home environment
3. Family life cycles
4. Life-changing events
5. Cultural, social, and situational environments
6. Utility
(Challenging, pp. 76-79)

90) What new trends are affecting consumer buyer behavior?

1. New attitudes and values
2. Time pressures
3. Cocooning
4. Indulgences and pleasure binges
5. Excitement and fantasy
6. Emphasis on health
7. Clanning
(Challenging, pp. 80-82)

CHAPTER 4
BUSINESS-to-BUSINESS BUYER BEHAVIOR

True-False Questions

1)   The Intel Pentium processor program is an example of a highly successful business-to-business selling operation.
     (True; Easy; pp. 90-92)

2)   International customers in business-to-business selling include importers, exporters, governments, and institutional customers.
     (True; Easy; p. 94)

3)   The business buying center is the group of individuals who make purchasing decisions.
     (True; Easy; p. 96)

4)   An influencer also serves as the gatekeeper in the business buying center.
     (False; Easy; p. 97)

5)   The gatekeeper is the individual who makes the eventual purchasing decision.
     (False; Easy; p. 97)

6)   Power relationships and personal objectives can affect business buying decisions.
     (True; Easy; pp. 99-100)

7)   A modified rebuy may occur when someone in the buying center believes vendors should be reevaluated.
     (True; Easy; p. 102)

8)   Exporters are companies that specialize in finding international customers for goods and services.
     (True; Moderate; p. 94)

9)   Governmental customers are not considered part of business-to-business selling operations.
     .   (False; Moderate, p. 94)

10)   Individuals within the buying center who shape the purchasing decision by providing information or criteria that should be used in evaluating alternatives are called influencers.
     (True; Moderate; p. 97)

11)   In the business buying center, buyers are given formal responsibility for making the purchase while deciders are the individuals who authorize those decisions.
     (True; Moderate; p. 97)

12) Various members of a buying center will have different degrees of cognitive involvement, depending on which role is being played.
(True; Moderate; pp. 99-100)

13) Selling to both consumers and businesses is known as dual-channel marketing.
(True; Moderate; p. 111)

14) The buying community is a group of buyers in a dual-channel marketing situation.
(False; Moderate; pp. 113-114)

15) Brand equity is a major concern for many business-to-business vendors, especially since CEOs are now making many of the business purchasing decisions.
(True; Moderate; p. 108)

16) William is the individual who examines a vendor's commitment to his firm and decides if the company doesn't have the technical competence to be effective, which means William is playing the role of procurement professional.
(True; Challenging; p. 106)

17) Most buying center members are able to avoid personality characteristics from affecting decisions by using decision rules called heuristics.
(False; Challenging; pp. 98-99)

18) Purchase terms following the selection of a vendor are often only a formality because the agreement has been worked out during the selection process.
(True; Challenging; p. 107)

19) Dual-channel marketing can create image problems for some organizations due to the transfer of image between markets.
(True; Challenging; p. 112)

20) Internet firms, such as Google, have changed the landscape of business-to-business vending since these companies allow for totally new purchasing approaches.
(True; Challenging; p. 111)

Multiple-Choice Questions

21) Intel succeeded in the business-to-business vending of its processors using which strategy?
   a) demand pull, based on name recognition
   b) supply push, based on low price
   c) co-demand, based on increased personal computer use
   d) cultural changes in perceptions of quality of U.S. manufacturers
(a; Easy; p. 92)

22) The fees paid to Olympic Committee members to place the 2002 games in Salt Lake City are an example of _____ .
    a) an ethical concern regarding bribes
    b) a social concern related to purchasing decisions
    c) an economic concern based on risk versus return
    d) an example of intrabusiness selling
(a; Easy; p. 105)

23) Which is not a business-to-business activity?
    a) vending process materials to manufacturers
    b) selling maintenance parts to end-user retail stores for resale
    c) selling operating supplies to another company
    d) reaching retail customers with a new marketing campaign
(d; Easy; p. 94)

24) A group of people who make a purchasing decision on behalf of a company is called _____ .
    a) the decision-makers
    b) the marketing team
    c) the institutional buyers
    d) the buying center
(d; Easy; p. 96)

25) Which member of the buyer center actually utilizes items that are purchased?
    a) users
    b) influencers
    c) deciders
    d) gatekeepers
(a; Easy; p. 96)

26) The members of the buying center who shape purchasing decisions by providing information and criteria are called _____ .
    a) users
    b) influencers
    c) deciders
    d) buyers
(b; Easy; p. 97)

27) The members of the buying center who authorize purchasing decisions are called _____ .
    a) users
    b) influencers
    c) deciders
    d) buyers
(c; Easy; p. 97)

28) The members of the buying center who control the flow of information and keep vendors in or out of the process are called _____ .
   a) users
   b) influencers
   c) deciders
   d) gatekeepers
(d; Easy; p. 97)

29) Which are social rules of behavior that affect how members of the buying center act?
   a) heuristics
   b) norms
   c) laws
   d) co-dependent variables
(b; Easy; p. 98)

30) Roles and perceived roles, motivational levels, and attitudes toward risk are examples of _____ factors that affect members of business buying centers.
   a) organizational
   b) individual
   c) cultural
   d) economic
(b; Easy; p. 99)

31) Comparing consensual versus authoritarian and individualistic decision styles in a region or country is an example of assessing _____ factors that affect members of business buying centers.
   a) organizational
   b) individual
   c) cultural
   d) nationalistic
(c; Easy; p. 101)

32) Decision rules that help employees make quick decisions regarding purchases are called _____ .
   a) heuristics
   b) satisficing
   c) methodologies
   d) role playing
(a; Easy; p. 98)

33) Spin-off sales occur when _____ .
   a) a person likes a business product so well she buys one for personal use
   b) advertising is combined with consumer promotions
   c) retailing is combined with wholesaling
   d) two related business buyers are identified by the vendor
(a; Easy; p. 112)

34) In the business-to-business buying process, the first step is _____ .
   a) identification of a need
   b) establishment of specifications
   c) identification of alternatives
   d) appointing a committee
(a; Easy; p. 103)

35) When evaluating vendors, an individual who helps assess vendors, commitment levels of those vendors, technical competence and other factors associated with the vendor is known as _____ .
   a) a marketing "hit man"
   b) a procurement professional
   c) a merchandiser
   d) a buying center operative
(b; Easy; p. 106)

36) When a firm's buying center agrees that defect rates for a purchased component part should be less than .01% of items received, the team is _____ .
   a) identifying needs
   b) establishing specifications
   c) evaluating vendors
   d) negotiating purchase terms
(b; Easy; p. 104)

37) Acme brick is able to sell products at prices that are 10% higher than competitors due to strong _____ .
   a) marketing myopia
   b) Internet integration
   c) brand equity in the Acme brand
   d) perceptions of brand parity
(c; Easy; p. 108)

38) Selling virtually the same goods or services to consumers and businesses is called _____ .
   a) relationship marketing
   b) double vending
   c) dual-channel marketing
   d) marketing extension
(c; Easy; p. 111)

39) Which is not typically a target in a media buy when business-to-business selling takes place?
   a) CEOs
   b) Board of Director members
   c) members of the top management team
   d) C-level members of the buying center
(b; Easy; p. 109)

40) An interlocking network of individual business owners, trade organizations, and others who make purchases together is called _____ .
   a) the buying center
   b) the buying community
   c) the purchasing group
   d) a consortium
(b; Easy; p. 113)

41) Internal marketing communications are messages sent to _____ .
   a) employees
   b) vendors
   c) buyers
   d) the government
(a; Easy; p. 116)

42) When Visa offers a discounted interest-rate credit card to members of the American Advertising Association based on a bulk subscription program, the company is providing a business-to-business _____ .
   a) good
   b) service
   c) assistance
   d) bribe
(b; Moderate; p. 94)

43) In a buying center, who would say, "Since I'm the one who actually has to use this product, you should listen to me."
   a) a user
   b) a buyer
   c) a decider
   d) a gatekeeper
(a; Moderate; p. 96)

44) In a buying center, who would say, "We need to limit our choices to local vendors."
   a) a user
   b) a buyer
   c) an influencer
   d) the gatekeeper
(c; Moderate; p. 97)

45) In a buying center for large companies, the purchasing agent is often _____ .
   a) the user
   b) the buyer
   c) the decider
   d) the gatekeeper
(b; Moderate; p. 97)

46) Which is <u>not</u> an individual factor that might influence a member of the buying center?
    a) personality features
    b) roles and perceived roles
    c) levels of cognitive involvement
    d) perceptions of economic conditions
(d; Moderate; p. 99)

47) A buying center member who wants more information and asks more questions when interacting with others is expressing _____ .
    a) a strong level of power
    b) risk averseness
    c) a strong level of cognitive involvement
    d) dominant personal objectives
(c; Moderate; p. 100)

48) A norm, such as to never buy from foreign suppliers due to the biases of the company's owner, is which kind of factor in buying decisions?
    a) pessimism
    b) individual
    c) cultural
    d) social
(d; Moderate; p. 101)

49) Which is a straight rebuy?
    a) re-ordering raw materials from the same vendor
    b) buying materials from a new vendor
    c) seeking bids from a new vendor because of dissatisfaction with the current supplier
    d) purchasing a new building for an expansion project
(a; Moderate; p. 101)

50) Which is a modified re-buy?
    a) becoming dissatisfied with a vendor and looking for new options
    b) re-ordering raw materials from the same vendor
    c) buying a new computer system
    d) purchasing a new building for an expansion project
(a; Moderate; p. 102)

51) Which is a new task purchasing decision?
    a) re-ordering from the same vendor
    b) ordering new materials from the same vendor
    c) upgrading the computer system
    d) buying a product or service for the first time
(d; Moderate; p. 102)

52) Which is derived demand?
   a) demand from consumers for new goods and services
   b) demand from manufacturers to find new customers
   c) demand linked to the production and sale of some other item
   d) demand as specified by governmental orders
   (c; Moderate; p. 103)

53) Which is related to the concept of derived demand?
   a) retail sales
   b) acceleration principle
   c) gatekeeping
   d) merchant distributorship
   (b; Moderate; p. 103)

54) The demand for automobile tires at a Ford factory is impacted by the supply of other component parts that go into the production of a Ford automobile illustrates the principle of _____ .
   a) derived demand
   b) acceleration principle
   c) joint demand
   d) brand equity
   (c; Moderate; p. 103)

55) Making the decision to outsource a certain component part occurs in which stage?
   a) identification of alternatives
   b) establishment of specifications
   c) identification of vendors
   d) selection of vendor(s)
   (a; Moderate, p. 104)

56) When members of the buying center agree to consider IBM, Compac, and Hewlett-Packard in purchasing new computers because they are the firms that expressed interest, they are in which stage of the buying process?
   a) establishment of specifications
   b) identification of alternatives
   c) identification of vendors
   d) evaluation of vendors
   (c; Moderate; p. 104)

57) When the buying center members find out that leasing a fleet from one car company has the advantage of a better repair service contract than other companies provide, they are in which stage?
   a) identification of needs
   b) establishment of specifications
   c) identification of alternatives
   d) evaluation of vendors
   (d; Moderate; pp. 105-106)

58) Selling personal computers to both retail stores and other businesses is _____ .
   a) multi-outlet marketing
   b) merchant distribution
   c) quantity enhancement marketing
   d) dual channel marketing
   (d; Moderate; p. 111)

59) A sales rep who likes his company car so well that he buys one for personal use is creating _____ .
   a) joint demand
   b) derived demand
   c) a spin-off sale
   d) a sale based on the acceleration principle
   (c; Moderate; p. 112)

60) Which is addressed to internal employees?
   a) internal marketing communications
   b) components of dual-channel marketing
   c) requests to build spin-off sales
   d) service agreements
   (a; Moderate; p. 116)

61) A person who joins the Kiwanis or Rotary club to make contacts for the purpose of getting better "buys" on various materials is part of _____ .
   a) an internal clique
   b) a buying community
   c) a marketing association
   d) an external vendor's agreement
   (b; Moderate; p. 114)

62) Which member of the buying center is most likely to negotiate the price?
   a) user
   b) influencer
   c) buyer
   d) gatekeeper
   (c; Challenging; p. 97)

63) Which member of the buying center is most likely to let the group know that some alternative companies have already been rejected?
    a) user
    b) influencer
    c) decider
    d) gatekeeper
(d; Challenging, p. 97)

64) Buying center members with higher levels of cognitive involvement will _____ .
    a) use the purchasing process to further personal power goals
    b) ask more questions during the purchasing process
    c) have no opinion about purchasing risk
    d) be most inclined to base a purchase decision on nepotism
(b; Challenging; p. 100)

65) Which individual factor in buying decision-making is also linked to risk perceptions, motives, and politics?
    a) level of power
    b) degree of tenure
    c) acceptance of company norms
    d) personal objectives
(d; Challenging; p. 100)

66) Which decision could be made most quickly?
    a) straight rebuy
    b) modified rebuy
    c) new task
    d) acceleration buy
(a; Challenging; p. 101)

67) A company that buys a product but only has limited or infrequent experience with that product will probably choose which path?
    a) straight rebuy
    b) modified rebuy
    c) new task purchase
    d) joint demand purchase
(b; Challenging; p. 102)

68) Which ordinarily would take the most time?
    a) straight rebuy
    b) modified rebuy
    c) new task purchase
    d) identifying a need
(c; Challenging; p. 102)

69) The linkage between steel and automobiles is _____ .
    a) derived demand
    b) co-demand
    c) joint demand
    d) fabricated demand
(a; Challenging; p. 103)

70) The acceleration principle explains how _____ .
    a) a small change in demand for cars creates a large change in demand for robotic machines that are used in the manufacturing of steel
    b) a small change in demand for steel creates a large change in demand for cars
    c) a product which sells well in the U.S. can sell quickly in foreign markets
    d) a merchant wholesaler can increase sales by contacting an agent retailer to form a relationship
(a; Challenging; p. 103)

71) The linkage between demand for car tires and car radios at automobile manufacturing plants is _____ .
    a) derived demand
    b) co-demand
    c) joint demand
    d) fabricated demand
(c; Challenging; p. 103)

72) An audit team is utilized in which stage of the buying process?
    a) identification of vendors
    b) evaluation of vendors
    c) selection of vendor(s)
    d) negotiating purchase terms
(b; Challenging; pp. 105-106)

73) It is typical for dual-channel marketing to begin with _____ .
    a) sales to businesses and later to consumers
    b) manufacturer demand for better component parts
    c) retailer demand for new products
    d) consumer demand for more purchasing options
(a; Challenging; p. 111)

74) Gathering valuable information about future sales by attending a conference or hearing a speech at a business seminar is part of _____ .
    a) internal marketing communications
    b) an external relationship marketing
    c) the buying community
    d) a global network
(c; Challenging; p. 114)

75) Buying community members gain the least amount of useful marketing information from
_____ .
   a) business associations such as the Kiwanis club
   b) speakers at business seminars
   c) other business owners
   d) business periodicals and local newspapers
(d; Challenging; p. 114)

76) An organizational factor that impacts the manner in which a purchase decision is made
would be_____ .
   a) the norms members of the buying center are expected to follow
   b) the risk involved in switching vendors
   c) the personalities of the sales staff and members of the buying center
   d) the capital assets a firm has available
(d; Challenging; p. 98)

77) In terms of management psychographics, a contented mensch is an individual who_____ .
   a) who works late every night and is constantly overloaded
   b) is trendy and shallow
   c) is devoted to home and family and who tries to get away from technology such as
      a Palm Pilot and cell phones
   d) is actively resistant to and intimidated by technology
(c; Challenging; p. 109)

78) Data mining by Volvo would allow for_____ .
   a) an increased focus on internal marketing
   b) the identification of buyer behavior patterns that can be matched to
      communication programs
   c) the development of a global brand
   d) the development of an effective website that can be used by influencers
(b; Challenging; p. 115)

79) The owner of a small company asks his secretary to call some of the local office supply
stores and locate two that would offer a good deal on a new copy machine. In performing
this task, the secretary is assuming the roles of _____ within the buying center.
   a) user and gatekeeper
   b) user and buyer
   c) user, decider and influencer
   d) buyer and gatekeeper
(a; Challenging; pp. 96-97)

80) Dan Johnson is heavily involved in the purchase of a new machine on his factory floor where is the foreman because he has a long-term goal of becoming the plant manager. His involvement in the purchase decision is an example of a(n)_____ .
   a) organizational influence
   b) individual influence
   c) cultural influence
   d) social influence
(d; Challenging; p. 98)

Short-Answer Questions

81) What types of individual goods are sold in business-to-business settings?

   1. Major equipment
   2. Accessory equipment
   3. Fabricated and component parts
   4. Process materials
   5. Maintenance or repair parts
   6. Operating supplies
   7. Raw materials
   8. Products for resale
(Moderate; p. 94)

82) Who are the potential customers for business-to-business sales?

   1. Manufacturing customers
   2. Governmental customers
   3. Institutional customers
   4. Wholesalers and distributor customers
   5. Retail customers
   6. International customers
(Moderate; p. 94)

83) Name and describe the members of a business buying center.

Users are the members of the organization who will actually use the good or service. Buyers are the individuals given the formal responsibility of making the purchase. Influencers are people who shape purchasing decisions by providing the information or criteria utilized in evaluating alternatives. Deciders are the individuals who authorize decisions. Gatekeepers control the flow of information to members of the buying center, keep people informed about potential alternatives and decision rules, and let people know when certain alternatives have been rejected.
(Moderate; pp. 96-97)

84)   What factors affect members of the buying center?

1. Organizational influences
2. Individual factors
3. Cultural factors
4. Social factors
(Moderate; p. 98)

85)   What individual factors can affect buying center members?

1. Personality features
2. Roles and perceived roles
3. Motivational levels
4. Levels of power
5. Attitudes toward risk
6. Levels of cognitive involvement
7. Personal objectives
(Challenging; pp. 99-101)

86)   What are the three categories of business-to-business sales decisions? Define each one.

1) A straight rebuy occurs when the firm has previously chosen a vendor and wishes to make a re-order. 2) A modified rebuy occurs when the company considers and evaluates alternatives on infrequent purchases. 3) A new task occurs when the company is buying a good or service for the first time and the company has no experience with the product.
(Moderate; pp. 101-102)

87)   What are the steps of the business-to-business buying process?

1. Identification of a need
2. Establishment of specifications
3. Identification of alternatives
4. Identification of vendors
5. Evaluation of vendors
6. Selection of vendors
7. Negotiation of purchase terms
(Moderate; p. 103)

88) Describe derived demand, the acceleration principle, and joint demand.

Derived demand is based on or linked to the production or sale of some other consumer good or service. The acceleration principle is that consumer demand for a product can dramatically increase or decrease the demand for equipment used in the manufacturing of that consumer product. Joint demand exists when demand for a particular product is influenced by the supply of other products used in a business or manufacturing of a new product.
(Challenging; pp. 103-104)

89) What is a buying community?

The buying community is an interlocking network of individual business owners, managers, trade organizations, social organizations, and firms that are used by small and medium-sized businesses to obtain information, provide assistance in making good business decisions, and develop relationships.
(Moderate; pp. 113-114)

90) What recent trends are present in the business-to-business buying environment?

1. Understanding the importance of a quality brand.
2. Following new trends in media selection, including print media and Internet usage.
3. Targeting media selection to the appropriate audience.
4. Making effective use of Internet programs.
(Challenging; pp. 115-116)

CHAPTER 5
PROMOTIONS OPPORTUNITY ANALYSIS

True-False Questions

1) One of the goals of a promotions' opportunity analysis is greater understanding of the target audience.
(True; Easy; p. 125)

2) A communications market analysis is the process of discovering the company's strengths and weaknesses in the area of marketing communications, along with an analysis of the environment.
(True; Easy; p. 126)

3) A competitive analysis identifies major suppliers for the firm.
(False; Easy; p. 126)

4) Positioning is the perception created in the consumer's mind regarding the nature of the competition and the external environment.
(False; Easy; p. 128)

5) The percentage of sales method is similar to the objective and task approach to communications' budgeting.
(False; Easy; p. 133)

6) Strategies are sweeping guidelines concerning the essence of the firm's short-term marketing activities and efforts.
(False; Easy; p. 136)

7) Segmentation is an effective method to identify target markets.
(True; Easy; p. 138)

8) Ordinarily, the first step of a promotions' opportunity analysis is the creation of a budget.
(False; Moderate; p. 125)

9) The steps of a promotions' opportunity analysis are similar to those of an overall IMC plan.
(True; Moderate; p.125)

10) Primary research involves searching the library for literature about the competition.
(False; moderate; p. 127)

11) An opportunity analysis involves an internal search for new marketing tactics.
(False; Moderate; p. 127)

12) Meet--the-competition budgeting is the most efficient form of communications budget.
(False; Moderate; p. 133)

13) A market segment is the general approach to differentiate the product to all customers in a geographic area.
(False; Moderate; p. 138)

14) Lower-level income families spend money primarily on sundries.
(False; Moderate; p. 141)

15) Geo-demographic segmentation is a combination of census data with psychographic information.
(True; Moderate; pp. 145-146)

16) An analysis of customers should include current company customers as well as potential new customers.
(True; Challenging; p. 128)

17) The percentage of sales method for budgeting tends to allocate funds for advertising at times directly opposite from when they are needed.
(True; Challenging; p. 133)

18) The two most general forms of market segments are current customers and potential customers.
(False; Challenging; p. 138)

19) The most effective medium to reach Generation X is television.
(False; Challenging; p. 145)

20) The NAICS code helps in geo-demographic segmentation programs.
(False; Challenging; p. 148)

Multiple-Choice Questions

21) Hallmark was able to widen the company's base of customers by _____ .
   a) adapting various lines of cards to target markets
   b) standardizing all products with the Hallmark brand
   c) standardizing cards within the United States, customizing internationally
   d) avoiding computer databases that would overcomplicate the selling process
(a; Easy, pp. 122-124)

22) A promotions' opportunity analysis is _____ .
   a) the process of identifying audiences for the goods and services the company sells
   b) any attempt by a company to promote products to consumers
   c) an analysis of the potential for new products and services
   d) a series of attempts to improve the promotion of the company through effective public relations

(a; Easy; p. 125)

23) A promotions' opportunity analysis should _____ .
   a) be concerned with product differentiation
   b) determine the promotional opportunities that exist for the company
   c) be unrelated to a target market
   d) focused only on short-range tactics

(b; Easy; p. 125)

24) A communications' market analysis is _____ .
   a) establishing communications' objectives
   b) defining marketing tactics
   c) creating a communications' marketing budget
   d) analysis of the company and its environment in terms of communication

(d; Easy; p. 126)

25) A competitive analysis _____ .
   a) often is not a component of a communications' marketing analysis
   b) relies on the development of new products to succeed
   c) identifies competitors and what they are doing in marketing communications
   d) does not consider global competitors

(c; Easy; p. 126)

26) A customer analysis is an extension of _____ .
   a) a target market analysis
   b) an opportunity analysis
   c) secondary data
   d) a competitive analysis

(a; Easy; p. 128)

27) Which of the following should not be studied in a customer analysis?
   a) current company customers
   b) the competition's customers
   c) manufacturers and suppliers
   d) potential customers

(c; Easy; p. 128)

28) The goal of an analysis of customers is _____ .
    a) to measure the impact of market segmentation
    b) to stress the importance of public relations
    c) to reveal customer interpretations of ads and marketing communications
    d) to differentiate the product in order to build brand equity
(c; Easy; p. 128)

29) The perception created in the consumer's mind regarding a company's products is _____ .
    a) secondary data
    b) an opportunity
    c) positioning
    d) competitive analysis
(c; Easy; p. 128)

30) A starting point that is studied in relation to the degree of change following a promotional campaign is a _____ .
    a) Post-hoc analysis
    b) marginal analysis
    c) benchmark measure
    d) standardized measure
(c; Easy, p. 130)

31) The early effects of an ad may be minimal, but over time gain momentum, according to the _____ model.
    a) diminishing returns
    b) threshold effects
    c) institutional purchasing
    d) purchase simulation
(b; Easy; p. 131)

32) The arbitrary allocation method is _____ .
    a) a form of positioning strategy
    b) a method of cost accounting
    c) a method of benchmarking advertising
    d) a budgeting approach
(d; Easy; p. 133)

33) One of the disadvantages of the meet-the-competition method of budgeting is _____ .
    a) marketing dollars may not be spent efficiently
    b) it leads to loss of market share
    c) when sales go down, so does spending
    d) it shows a lack of commitment to marketing
(a; Easy; p. 133)

34) Sweeping guidelines concerning the essence of a company's marketing efforts are _____.
   a) tactics
   b) strategies
   c) quality control
   d) benefit segmentation
(b; Easy; p. 136)

35) A set of businesses or groups of individual consumers with distinct characteristics is _____.
   a) a consumer group
   b) demographics
   c) a market segment
   d) manufacturers
(c; Easy; p. 138)

36) Market segments should be internally _____.
   a) heterogeneous
   b) high frequency
   c) variable
   d) homogenous
(d; Easy; p. 138)

37) Ethnic groups tend to _____.
   a) be less brand loyal
   b) put less value on quality
   c) value relationships to companies that serve them
   d) be primarily concerned with price
(c; Easy; p. 143)

38) Geodemographics _____.
   a) combines census data with psychographic data
   b) segments populations by generations
   c) is a form of global marketing
   d) groups consumers by region
(a; Easy; pp. 145-146)

39) Which method is used to decipher the industries that contain potential business customers?
   a) NAICS
   b) the Better Business Bureau
   c) primary data
   d) geodemographics
(a; Easy; p. 148)

40) The Food Network discovers that the company's competitors are viewed as more exciting through which process?
   a) target market analysis
   b) competitive analysis
   c) differentiation analysis
   d) strengths and weakness analysis
   (b; Moderate; pp. 126-127)

41) Which is not a source of secondary data?
   a) a trip to a competitor's store
   b) advertisements by competitors
   c) a prospectus
   d) an annual report
   (a; Moderate; pp. 126-127)

42) A company discovers senior citizens are not being reached by company advertising, using which process?
   a) opportunity analysis
   b) strategy analysis
   c) analysis of primary data
   d) analysis of publicity
   (a; Moderate; p. 127)

43) Mountain Dew confirms that the product is considered more hip and trendy than Coke through which process?
   a) analysis of primary data
   b) analysis of market segments
   c) analysis of positioning
   d) analysis of secondary data
   (c; Moderate; p. 128)

44) When a concave downward function is present, increasing advertising expenditures result in _____ .
   a) greater sales
   b) diminishing returns
   c) average returns
   d) further advertising expenditures
   (b; Moderate; p. 132)

45) Even though Montgomery Wards went out of business, a few consumers still recall the company when thinking about making a new washing machine purchase due to _____ .
   a) Carry-over effects of previous ads
   b) Wear-out effects of ads of competitors
   c) threshold effects of former ads
   d) decay effects of former ads
   (a; Moderate; p. 132)

46) Which is the most effective method of achieving specific company advertising goals?
 a) objective and task
 b) percentage of sales
 c) what we can afford
 d) payout planning
(a; Moderate; p. 134)

47) Burger King decides to match McDonald's dollar-for-dollar in advertising. Which approach is being used?
 a) objective and task
 b) meet the competition
 c) what we can afford
 d) the percentage of share method
(b; Moderate; p. 133)

48) If Tang breakfast drink focuses on changing its image to a more current and "hip" image, this is an example of a _____ .
 a) a percentage-of-sales budgeting method
 b) a communications' strategy
 c) a competitive analysis
 d) a communications' tactic
(b; Moderate; p. 136)

49) Coupon programs are an example of _____ .
 a) a strategy
 b) tactics
 c) geo-demographic analysis
 d) collecting secondary data
(b; Moderate; p. 137)

50) Analysis of buying patterns by gender is an example of _____ .
 a) a strategy
 b) collecting secondary data
 c) a market segmentation approach
 d) an opportunity analysis
(c; Moderate; pp. 138-141)

51) For a market segment to be viable, it should _____ .
 a) differ from the population as a whole
 b) be heterogeneous
 c) contain many demographics
 d) contain sub-segments
(a; Moderate; p. 138)

52) Level of educational completion is an example of segmentation by _____ .
   a) pyschographics
   b) generations
   c) demographics
   d) geodemographics
(c; Moderate; p. 139)

53) A senior citizen who has withdrawn from society and tends to isolate himself from others is called _____ .
   a) a healthy indulger
   b) a frail recluse
   c) a healthy hermit
   d) an ailing outgoer
(c; Moderate; p. 142)

54) A television set, VCR, or personal computer would be examples of a _____ .
   a) necessity item
   b) sundry item
   c) luxury item
   d) demographic item
(b; Moderate; pp. 141-142)

55) A person born in 1948 who went to Woodstock, campaigned for Robert Kennedy, and is now an account executive would be _____ .
   a) Boomers I
   b) Generation Y
   c) Depression cohort
   d) Generation Z
(a; Moderate; p. 145)

56) In terms of b-to-b business segmentation, based on the purchase decision process, Foot Locker, which regularly buys all brands of shoes, would be considered a _____ by Nike and Reebok.
   a) novice
   b) sophisticate
   c) first time prospect
   d) geo-demographic segment
(b; Moderate; p. 150)

57) In terms of b-to-b business segmentation, based on the purchase decision pro, which have never purchased an item and are evaluating vendors?
   a) First-time prospects
   b) novices
   c) sophisticates
   d) rookies
(a; Moderate; p. 150)

58) A quality global marketing communications analysis would <u>not</u> include _____ .
   a) identification of strengths and weaknesses of local competitors
   b) segmentation programs
   c) literal translations of ads
   d) studies of norms, beliefs, and laws
   (c; Moderate; pp. 151-152)

59) Which person provides assistance in understanding a local region?
   a) the company's president
   b) the creative
   c) the cultural assimilator
   d) a regional advisor
   (c; Moderate; p. 152)

60) Suppose Foot Locker has determined that the company is <u>not</u> effectively reaching Generation Y. Which process was used?
   a) target market analysis
   b) competitive analysis
   c) analysis of primary data
   d) analysis of secondary data
   (a; Challenging; p. 128)

61) Discovering that the way to reach Generation Y is through the Internet is accomplished using which method?
   a) a competitive analysis
   b) a positioning analysis
   c) an analysis of customers
   d) an analysis of secondary data
   (c; Challenging; p. 128)

62) A local video rental store decides to develop a program to increase customer traffic in the summer. Which is being performed?
   a) communications budget
   b) target market analysis
   c) positioning
   d) creating a marketing communications objective
   (d; Challenging; p. 136)

63) If a company rejects a budgeting method because it would take too long to prepare, odds are the budget is called _____ .
   a) percentage of sales
   b) meet the competition
   c) what we can afford
   d) objective and task
   (d; Challenging; p. 134)

64) Which budgeting method would utilize Nielsen ratings?
   a) arbitrary allocation
   b) meet-the-competition
   c) payout planning
   d) quantitative models
   (c; Challenging; p. 134)

65) Which is not a tactic?
   a) selling gift certificates
   b) creating purchase bonus programs
   c) changing prices
   d) presenting a young, trendy image
   (d; Challenging; p. 137)

66) Susan is classified as an ailing outgoing senior citizen because _____ .
   a) she resembles a baby boomer
   b) she has major health problems
   c) she is more spiritual than her friends
   d) she is isolated from medical care
   (b; Challenging; p. 143)

67) Which group is most likely to express concerns about balancing family and work?
   a) females
   b) Generation X
   c) Generation Y
   d) males
   (a; Challenging; p. 139)

68) A commercial showing the luxury and quality of a Lexus is based on _____ .
   a) geographic segmentation
   b) income segmentation
   c) ethnic segmentation
   d) geo-demographic segmentation
   (b; Challenging; pp. 141-142)

69) An excellent medium for marketing to geographic segments is _____ .
   a) regional magazines
   b) Internet outlets
   c) national television
   d) palm pilots
   (a; Challenging; p. 145)

70) PRIZM is a company that specializes in _____ .
a) product differentiation
b) geodemographics
c) price segmentation
d) benefit segmentation
(b; Challenging; p. 146)

71) A shift in advertising that shows the benefits of the product rather than a focus on the customers is called _____ .
a) demographic segmentation
b) psychographic segmentation
c) benefit segmentation
d) business-to-business segmentation
(c; Challenging; pp. 146-147)

72) A company discovers that its stores located in urban areas must offer products which are somewhat different from those in the suburbs used _____ .
a) demographic segmentation
b) psychographics
c) competitive analysis
d) geographic segmentation
(d; Challenging; p. 145)

73) If Microsoft attempted to use a different communications' approach when designing mailings for various business industries, it could utilize _____ .
a) the NAICS code
b) demographics
c) competitive analysis
d) opportunity analysis
(a; Challenging; p. 148)

74) A new organization is looking for a hotel to accommodate a major sales meeting. This organization, in terms of the purchase decision process segmentation approach, is _____ .
a) a first-time prospect
b) a novice
c) a sophisticate
d) a marketing objective
(a; Challenging; p. 150)

75) Stopping an ad which appears to be funny in one culture but offensive in another is probably performed by _____ .
a) a creative
b) a bilingual
c) a cultural assimilator
d) the local government
(c; Challenging; p. 152)

76) An inventory software producer found that no one was producing software to handle inventory for salvage yards. This information would have mostly likely been gathered during the _____ .
   a) competitive analysis
   b) target market analysis
   c) opportunity analysis
   d) customer analysis
(c; Challenging; p. 127)

77) Manufacturers of appliances, such as GE and Whirlpool, advertise on a continuous basis since appliances are purchased only when they are needed. To ensure the brand name is remembered when the need arises, these manufacturers are relying on _____ .
   a) threshold effects
   b) sales-response function curve
   c) wear out effects
   d) carryover effect
(d; Challenging; p. 132)

78) Typically, the percentage of the communications budget used for media advertising is _____ .
   a) 25%
   b) 50%
   c) 75%
   d) 100%
(a; Challenging; p. 154)

79) The country with the highest level of advertising expenditures is _____ .
   a) the United States
   b) Japan
   c) Germany
   d) United Kingdom
(a; Challenging; p. 135)

80) Marketing insurance to individuals who rent an apartment is an example of segmentation based on _____ .
   a) demographics
   b) usage
   c) benefits
   d) geodemographics
(a; Challenging; p. 140)

Short-Answer Questions

81)   What are the steps in a promotions' opportunity analysis?

1. Complete a communications marketing analysis
2. Establish objectives
3. Create a budget
4. Prepare a strategy
5. Match tactics with strategy

(Moderate; pp. 125-126)

82)   What are the five components of a communications' market analysis?

1. A competitive analysis
2. An opportunity analysis
3. A target market analysis
4. An analysis of customers
5. An analysis of positioning

(Moderate; p. 126)

83)   What customer groups should be considered during the customer analysis?

1. Current company customers
2. The competition's customers
3. Potential customers who may become interested

(Moderate: p. 128)

84)   Identify the various methods that can be used to develop a communications budget?

1. Percentage of sales
2. Meet-the-competition
3. What we can afford
4. Objective and task
5. Payout planning
6. Quantitative models

(Moderate; pp. 133-134)

85)   Describe the difference between strategies and tactics.

Strategies are sweeping guidelines concerning the essence of a company's long-term marketing efforts. Tactics are the things companies do to support strategies in the shorter term.

(Moderate; pp. 136-139)

86) What are the major segmentation strategies used in consumer markets?

1. Demographics
2. Psychographics
3. Generations
4. Geographic
5. Geodemographic
6. Benefit
7. Usage
(Moderate; p. 139)

87) What are the methods of segmenting business-to-business markets?

1. NAICS/SIC codes
2. Business type
3. Business size
4. Geographic location
5. Product usage
6. Purchase decision process
7. Customer value
(Moderate; p. 148)

88) One method of s segmenting business-to-business markets is by the purchase decision process. Identify the characteristics of each segment using this approach.

1) First-time prospects are companies that have never purchased a particular product or service, but have started evaluating vendors. 2) Novices are first-time customers who have made a recent purchase of a product or service. 3) Sophisticates are companies that have already purchased the product and are ready to rebuy or have just made repeat purchases.
(Challenging; p. 150)

89) What are the characteristics of a viable market segment?

1. The individuals within the segment should be similar, i.e. homogenous.
2. The segment should differ from the population as a whole.
3. The segment must be large enough to be financially viable when targeted by a separate marketing campaign.
4. The segment must be reachable through some type of media or marketing communications method.
(Challenging; pp. 138-139)

90)   What is an opportunity analysis? What are some typical questions that should be asked during an opportunity analysis?

This is an analysis to see what type of communications' opportunities may exist for a particular product. Typical questions that can be asked include:
1. Are there customers that the competition is ignoring or not serving?
2. Which markets are heavily saturated and have intense competition?
3. Are the benefits of our goods and services being clearly articulated to our customers?
4. Are there opportunities, using a slightly different marketing approach, to build relationships with customers?
5. Are there opportunities that are not being pursued or is our brand positioned with a cluster of other companies in such a manner that it cannot stand out?
(Challenging; pp. 127-128)

CHAPTER 6
ADVERTISING MANAGEMENT

True-False Questions

1) A message theme is the outline of the key ideas that an advertising program is supposed to convey.
(True; Easy; p. 163)

2) A media service company negotiates and purchases media packages, which are also known as media buys.
(True; Easy; p. 168)

3) Reference requests are not usually made during the selection of an advertising agency, especially for finalist companies.
(False; Easy; pp. 171-172)

4) A stewardship report is an update on the work performed on an advertising campaign as prepared by the advertising agency.
(True; Easy; p. 175)

5) A top-of-mind brand is the brand that creates the impression that it is the easiest to buy.
(False; Easy; p. 179)

6) When ads are combined with other marketing efforts into a larger, more integrated effort revolving around a theme, it is known as a promotional campaign.
(True; Easy; p. 181)

7) A flighting approach to advertising is a year-round level budget method.
(False; Easy; p. 182)

8) Advertising is separate from the traditional promotions mix since it focuses on the end user.
(False; Moderate; p. 163)

9) When the majority of a company's advertising budget is spent on media buys, rather than producing the advertisement, the company should be inclined to work in-house.
(True; Moderate; p. 167)

10) A boutique agency is one that provides a full range of advertising services.
(False; Moderate; p. 168)

11) One method to measure the creative reputation and capability of an advertising agency is to look at a list of awards the company has received for past campaigns.
(True; Moderate; p. 171)

12) During the product-specific research phase of advertising planning, an agency asks consumers if there are any problems or difficulties with the product.
(True; Moderate; p. 173)

13) A top-choice brand is the one that the customer ordinarily recalls in his or her evoked set when making a purchase decision.
(True; Moderate; p. 179)

14) A pulsating schedule of advertising involves continuous advertising with bursts of higher intensity during specific periods of the year.
(True; Moderate; p. 182)

15) A disclaimer warranty describes the shelf life of a product.
(False; Moderate; p. 185)

16) Winning a variety of advertising awards for creativity assures a company that the agency can be objective in developing a campaign.
(False; Challenging; p. 171)

17) If Target discovers that most people view the company as comparable to JC Penney's and other upscale retail outlets, it probably gained the information through an analysis of positioning.
(True; Challenging; p. 178)

18) When a consumer is asked which brand of razor he is most inclined to buy, the individual will respond with a top-choice brand.
(True; Challenging; p. 179)

19) Toy companies and diet food companies have one thing in common: they are likely to use continuous campaign schedules in advertising.
(False; Challenging; p. 182)

20) The Surgeon General's warning on a pack of cigarettes is an example of an advertising constraint component of the creative brief.
(True; Challenging; p. 185)

Multiple-Choice Questions

21) A message theme is _____ .
   a) a form of leverage point
   b) the media choices a company makes
   c) the key idea(s) an advertisement conveys
   d) the type of appeal that is used in an advertisement
(c; Easy; p. 163)

22) The key ideas contained in an advertisement are referred to as _____ .
   a) the message theme
   b) the appeal
   c) the executional framework
   d) the leverage point
(a; Easy; p. 163)

23) The major principle guiding an advertising program should be _____ .
   a) personality
   b) complexity
   c) conversation
   d) consistency
(d; Easy; p. 164)

24) Which is <u>not</u> a decision variable used in selecting an external agency versus creating advertisements in-house?
   a) the objectivity factor
   b) the spokesperson factor
   c) the complexity of the product
   d) the creativity issue
(b; Easy; p. 167)

25) The 75/15/10 breakdown means _____ .
   a) 75% is spent on media time or space
   b) 75% is spend on ad production
   c) 75% is spent on the creative budget
   d) 75% of the advertisement is complete before billing
(a; Easy; p. 167)

26) A boutique _____ .
   a) is the largest form of agency
   b) only creates television ads
   c) serves in-house clients
   d) offers one specialized service or works with one type of client
(d; Easy; p. 168)

27) A media service company _____ .
   a) negotiates contract rates between the agency and the client
   b) negotiates pay rates for creatives and advertising performers
   c) negotiates and purchases media packages
   d) handles direct marketing efforts
(c; Easy; p. 168)

28) Media buys are normally made by _____ .
   a) the creative
   b) the account executive
   c) the traffic manager
   d) a media service company
(d; Easy; p. 168)

29) Which is a conflict of interest problem in the selection of an advertising agency?
   a) the advertising agency is owned by a larger company
   b) the advertising agency already represents a similar product or company
   c) the advertising agency outsources creative work
   d) the creative works for more than one client
(b; Easy; p. 170)

30) A communications market analysis does not include _____ .
   a) a competitive analysis
   b) a target market analysis
   c) an economic forecasting analysis
   d) an analysis of customers
(c; Easy; pp. 177-178)

31) An analysis of positioning is designed to _____ .
   a) explain how the firm and its products are perceived relative to competitors
   b) explain the buying habits of various consumers
   c) evaluate past advertising campaigns and their effects on sales
   d) provide the information need to prepare a creative brief
(a; Easy; p. 178)

32) A top-of-mind brand is _____ .
   a) the company's chief competitor, as identified by a competitive analysis
   b) the brand that comes to mind in a product category
   c) the most expensive good or service in a product category
   d) a purchasing alternative when the primary product is not available
(b; Easy; p. 179)

33) Communication and advertising objectives typically do not include _____ .
   a) providing information
   b) persuasion
   c) supporting other marketing efforts
   d) notifying the public of a product recall
(d; Easy; p. 179)

34) A pulsating schedule of advertising _____ .
   a) involves continuous advertising with bursts of higher intensity
   b) seeks consumer input into ideal times to advertise
   c) is level throughout the year
   d) is not a common form of advertising schedule due to costs
   (a; Easy; p. 182)

35) A flighting approach to advertising _____ .
   a) is based solely on the client's overall budget
   b) is level throughout the year
   c) is advertising only during one month of the year
   d) is advertising only during certain parts of the year
   (d; Easy; p. 182)

36) The advertising support component of the creative brief includes _____ .
   a) media selection and media buys
   b) the creative brief's constraint component
   c) the nature of the advertising appeal
   d) the facts which substantiate a unique selling point
   (d; Easy; p. 185)

37) Which is typically not a component of a creative brief?
   a) the economic factors affecting company sales
   b) the objective of the campaign
   c) the target market for the campaign
   d) the message theme
   (a; Easy; pp. 183-185)

38) A disclaimer warranty typically does not specify _____ .
   a) the conditions under which a warranty will be honored
   b) past legal actions which have been taken
   c) potential hazards associated with products
   d) the terms of financing agreements, bonuses, and discounts
   (b; Moderate; p. 185)

39) One disadvantage of an in-house ad agency is _____ .
   a) the company may go stale or fail to recognize new opportunities
   b) the cost
   c) morale within the marketing department may be lower
   d) greater potential for lawsuits
   (a; Moderate; pp. 166-167)

40) In a 75/15/10 breakdown, 10% is spent on _____ .
   a) media buys
   b) creative salary
   c) actual production of the ad
   d) advertising agency selection
   (c; Moderate; p. 167)

41) The "whole egg theory" used by Young and Rubicam _____ .
   a) heavily utilized boutique agencies
   b) was only offered to small clients
   c) was designed to help the client achieve total success
   d) was a new type of public relations program
   (c; Moderate; p. 169)

42) A conflict of interest would appear when _____ .
   a) the client company's leaders cannot decide which ad agency to select
   b) the ad agency already represents a similar product
   c) the client company employs several former members of the ad agency
   d) the ad agency employs several former members of the client company
   (b; Moderate; p. 170)

43) Personal chemistry is a selection factor that should _____ .
   a) be examined early in the selection process
   b) never affect the choice, which should only be made rationally
   c) determine if an in-house agency should be chosen
   d) be considered in the final stages of selection
   (d; Moderate; p. 171)

44) The "got milk" campaign emerged after consumers were deprived of milk for a week. This form of research is known as _____ .
   a) product specific
   b) market specific
   c) consumer specific
   d) quantitative
   (a; Moderate; p. 173)

45) Someone who believes he or she is always on the cutting edge of fashion can be identified using _____ .
   a) product specific research
   b) a major selling idea
   c) the Values and Life Style Model (VALS)
   d) quantitative research
   (c; Moderate; p. 174)

46) A stewardship report describes _____ .
   a) how an advertising agency is selected
   b) how the client has developed its advertising budget
   c) the nature of a company's public relations program
   d) the process of developing an advertising campaign for the client
(d; Moderate; p. 175)

47) Which reveals a company's strengths and weaknesses in the marketplace?
   a) competitive analysis
   b) opportunity analysis
   c) target market analysis
   d) positioning analysis
(b; Moderate; pp. 177-178)

48) A customer who reports that Lexus is the first car he thinks of in the "luxury automobile" category is describing _____ .
   a) a top-of-mind brand
   b) a top-choice brand
   c) a quality choice brand
   d) a top-of-industry brand
(a; Moderate; p. 179)

49) A customer who buys Coke and Pepsi all the time, and no other brands, holds these two products as _____ .
   a) quality brands
   b) price brands
   c) top-choice brands
   d) continuous choices
(c; Moderate; p. 179)

50) Which company is most likely going to use a continuous campaign schedule of advertising?
   a) a lawn mower manufacturer
   b) a Christmas decoration supplier
   c) a beer distributor
   d) a space heater manufacturer
(c; Moderate; p. 182)

51) A flighting campaign is best suited to products with _____ .
   a) one key peak season and an off season
   b) a series of small seasons and no off seasons
   c) a series of customers who buy at different times during the year
   d) services
(a; Moderate; p. 182)

52) A pulsating schedule is used for products that have _____ .
    a) steady sales throughout the year
    b) peak seasons but do sell throughout the entire year
    c) primarily governmental customers
    d) low inventories in stock
(b; Moderate; p. 182)

53) Which company would be most likely to use a right-brained emotional advertising campaign?
    a) a florist
    b) a financial services company
    c) a newspaper
    d) an office furniture company
(a; Moderate; pp. 184-185)

54) A business-to-business office furniture company's approach to advertising is most likely to be _____ .
    a) right brained
    b) left brained
    c) full brained
    d) whole hearted
(b; Moderate; pp. 184-185)

55) A creative brief is not likely to include _____ .
    a) an objective of building brand image
    b) a target audience clearly specified
    c) a public relations' program in detail
    d) a clear message theme
(c; Moderate; pp. 183-185)

56) Which product is most likely to include a disclaimer warranty?
    a) medicine
    b) shirt
    c) hammer
    d) scotch tape
(a; Moderate; p. 185)

57) Which product is least likely to require a disclaimer warranty?
    a) automobile
    b) airline travel
    c) athletic socks
    d) chewing tobacco
(c; Moderate; p. 195)

58) Which is a message theme?
   a) We want to beat the competition.
   b) We want to increase sales.
   c) We want our customers to think of us as the high volume, low-price leader.
   d) We want to develop new goods and services for future consumer needs right now.
   (c; Challenging; p. 163)

59) Which presents the biggest problem for a company wishing to advertise?
   a) being a large account seeking a major advertising agency
   b) being a complex product manufacturer seeking to use an external agency
   c) being able to spend 75% of the company's budget for advertising on media buys
   d) finding an agency which is more objective than an in-house program
   (b; Challenging; p. 167)

60) Before examining possible advertising agencies, it is important to finalize the process of selection as well as the criteria that will be used in the selection process _____ .
   a) because agencies need to know the selection process and selection criteria
   b) to prevent personal biases from affecting the decision
   c) to ensure that full-service agencies are selected
   d) to determine if an external agency will be used or the work will be done in-house
   (b; Challenging; p.170)

61) An agency representing a client selling car batteries who has previously created ads for a company selling tires would have _____ .
   a) relevant experience
   b) a conflict of interest
   c) interpersonal chemistry
   d) company complexity
   (a; Challenging; p. 170)

62) An oral presentation by an advertising agency seeking a new client should _____ .
   a) reveal how the agency would deal with specific issues in preparing the campaign
   b) nearly always be presented by a heavy hitter
   c) be refused because the client company has not clarified its selection criteria
   d) be the first step in the selection process
   (a; Challenging; p. 172)

63) The account executive does not _____ .
   a) work with the creative brief
   b) serve as a liaison between the client and the agency
   c) typically prepare ad copy
   d) negotiate contracts
   (c; Challenging; pp. 174-175)

64) If Ralph Lauren's wants to determine if the brand will appeal to a cohort group that is rich, elite, and distinct, which method would reveal such a trend?
   a) product specific research
   b) personal drive analysis
   c) assessment of the major selling idea
   d) a sociological approach assessing social class
(d; Challenging; pp. 173-174)

65) An individual's desire to drink high quality wine as an expression of individuality and taste is discovered using _____ .
   a) product specific research
   b) direct observation (anthropology)
   c) mood assessment techniques
   d) a personal drive analysis approach
(d; Challenging; pp. 173-174)

66) A communications market analysis should reveal _____ .
   a) the nature of the product
   b) the message theme
   c) the media usage habits of the target market
   d) the optimal advertising budget
(c; Challenging; pp. 177-178)

67) Understanding that BMW is perceived as the quality leader results from _____ .
   a) communications market analysis
   b) analysis of customers
   c) analysis of position
   d) opportunities analysis
(c; Challenging; p. 178)

68) Finding out that your company's advertisements are viewed negatively by a large portion of your business's buyers results from _____ .
   a) communications market analysis
   b) competitive analysis
   c) analysis of position
   d) analysis of customers
(d; Challenging; p. 178)

69) A brand that is both top of mind and top choice reflects _____ .
   a) a high degree of brand parity
   b) a high level of brand equity
   c) brand availability
   d) distinct private branding
(b; Challenging; p. 179)

70) In business-to-business situations, being top of mind or top choice is most important in
_____ .
a) modified rebuy situations
b) reorders
c) straight rebuy situations
d) vendor support programs
(a; Challenging; p. 179)

71) In terms of the communications' budget schedule, diet services, such as Jenny Craig and
Weight Watchers, would ordinarily use _____ .
a) continuous advertising schedules
b) a pulsating schedule
c) a derivative advertising schedule
d) a flighting schedule
(b; Challenging; p. 182)

72) The milk mustache in the "got milk" campaign reflects _____ .
a) the ad's executional framework
b) the leverage point of the ad
c) a message theme
d) the ad's appeal
(b; Challenging; p. 163)

73) In terms of the creative brief, an endorsement by eight out of 10 doctors recommending a
product is a form of _____ .
a) disclaimer
b) message theme
c) support
d) constraint
(c; Challenging; p. 185)

74) For a creative brief, constraints do <u>not</u> include _____ .
a) Left-brained approaches
b) disclaimers
c) copyright registrations
d) trademarks
(a; Challenging; p. 185)

75) Women over the age of 40 _____ .
a) have less buying power than women under 40
b) tend to have a lower level of self-assurance than women under 40
c) are a key focus for most advertising campaigns directed at females
d) are inclined to make purchases that reflect affluence, self-indulgence and comfort
(d; Challenging pp. 160-161)

76) For a creative brief, the target audience information should contain_____ .
   a) only basic demographic information, such as gender and age
   b) information about the users of a particular product
   c) not only demographic information, but also psychographic information and any other information that will help the creative better understand the target audience
   d) past purchase behavior of every company or consumer that has purchased the product in addition to the demographic information
   (c; Challenging; pp. 183-184)

77) An advertisement that incorporates a coupon for 50 cents is designed to meet the communications' objective of _____ .
   a) encouraging action
   b) building brand image
   c) providing information
   d) persuading consumers to purchase immediately
   (a; Challenging; pp. 178-181)

78) The scheduling of all of the activities required to build an advertising campaign from designing ads to producing the ads is the responsibility of the _____ .
   a) account executive
   b) creative
   c) traffic manager
   d) brand manager
   (c; Challenging; p. 176)

79) Questions that companies should ask about an ad agency's production capabilities and media purchasing capabilities include all of the following except?
   a) Does the agency buy efficiently?
   b) Is the agency able to negotiate special rates and publication positions?
   c) Does the agency routinely get "bumped" by higher-paying firms so ads do not run at highly desirable times?
   d) Does the agency use a media service company to purchase television time?
   (d; Challenging; p. 171)

80) If a company's media budget numbers are 85-10-5 and uses an external ad agency, this means the company _____ .
   a) is spending too much money on creative work
   b) should continue using an external advertising agency
   c) should discontinue using an external agency and do the work inhouse
   d) is spending too much money on media buys
   (b; Challenging; p. 167)

Short-Answer Questions

81)   What is a message theme? What does it reflect?

A message theme is an outline of the key idea(s) that the advertising program is supposed to convey. It should reflect the overall IMC theme.
(Easy; p. 163)

82)   Describe the work of the creative in creating an advertising campaign.

Creatives are the persons who actually develop and produce advertisements.
(Easy, p. 175)

83)   Name and describe other types of agencies that serve client firms, besides advertising agencies.

Media service companies negotiate and purchase media packages or media buys. Direct marketing agencies handle direct marketing campaigns. Sales or trade promotions companies provide assistance in creating attention-getting mechanisms. Public relations firms help companies develop positive images and deal with negative publicity.
(Moderate; p. 168)

84)   Discuss the difference between deception and puffery.

Puffery is the use of an exaggerated claim about a product without making an overt attempt to deceive or mislead. A deceptive advertisement gives a typical person a false impression or presents false information that results in a favorable attitude towards the product and the purchase or intent to purchase the product being advertised.
(Moderate: p. 180)

85)   Name the steps involved in selecting an advertising agency.

1. Set goals
2. Select criteria
3. Request references
4. View oral and written presentations
5. Meet key personnel
6. Make the selection and finalize the contract
7. Notify all parties
(Moderate; p. 169)

86)   What roles do advertising account executives play in developing campaigns?

The advertising account executive is the key go-between for the agency and the client company. The executive solicits the account, finalizes the details of the contract, works

with the creative department that will prepare the campaign, and helps the client company refine and define its major message.
(Moderate; pp. 174-175)

87) Name the elements of a creative brief.

- The objective
- The target audience
- The message theme
- The support
- The constraints

(Moderate; 183)

88) Name the steps of advertising campaign management.

1. Review the communications market analysis.
2. Establish communications' objectives consistent with those developed in a Promotions Opportunity Analysis program.
3. Review the communications budget.
4. Select the media in conjunction with the advertising agency.
5. Review the information with the advertising creative in the creative brief.

(Challenging; p. 177)

89) For the creative brief, name the most common objectives of an advertisement.

- Increase brand awareness
- Build brand image
- Increase customer traffic
- Increase retailer or wholesaler orders
- Increase inquiries from end-users and channel members
- Provide information

(Challenging; p. 183)

90) Name and describe the five most common decision variables in the selection of an in-house versus external advertising agency.

1. The size of the account, which should match the client to the agency.
2. The money that can be spent on media, which should be 75% of the budget.
3. The objectivity factor, recognizing that an agency can be more objective.
4. The complexity of a product, where more complex products are better understood internally.
5. The creativity issue, agencies are usually more creative in their approach.

(Challenging; p. 167)

CHAPTER 7
ADVERTISING DESIGN
THEORETICAL FRAMEWORKS AND TYPES OF APPEALS

True-False Questions

1) There is a sequential set of steps that leads to a purchase, according to the hierarchy of effects model.
    (True; Easy; p. 195)

2) The first stage in the hierarchy of effects model is awareness.
    (True; Easy; p. 195)

3) Means-end theory is the basis of the MECCAS approach to advertising.
    (True; Easy; p. 197)

4) A means-end chain stresses the linkage between a product's attributes and its price.
    (False; Easy; p. 197)

5) Fear is an ineffective form of advertising appeal that has been largely abandoned.
    (False; Easy; p. 202)

6) Sex appeals and nudity tend to increase attention to advertisements, but only for males.
    (False; Easy; pp. 208-209)

7) Rational appeals are most effective when consumers have high levels of involvement and are willing to pay attention to the ad.
    (True; Easy; p. 215)

8) Executional frameworks are a key ingredient in a MECCAS model.
    (True; Moderate; p. 197)

9) Visual images tend to be more difficult to remember than verbal copy.
    (False; Moderate; p. 199)

10) Visual esperanto is the development of an image than readily translates across cultures, but only with certain languages, such as Spanish.
    (False; Moderate; p. 200)

11) Severity and vulnerability are key elements in rational advertisements.
    (False; Moderate; p. 202)

12) Humor and sexuality go well together in advertisements in all cultures.
    (False; Moderate; p. 211)

13) Controversial sexual ads are interesting to viewers, but sometimes fail to transmit key information that will be recalled.
(True; Moderate; p. 209)

14) Scarcity appeals are designed to raise prices.
(False; Moderate; p. 218)

15) A shopper who sees an item in a store, becomes intrigued, asks for information, and then makes a purchase is following the sequence of the hierarchy of effects model.
(True; Challenging; pp. 195-196)

16) The hierarchy of effects model follows a pathway that is similar to the sequence of cognitive, affective, and conative components.
(True; Challenging; p. 196)

17) Low levels of fear in an ad may not create feelings of severity or vulnerability.
(True; Challenging; p. 203)

18) When humor in an ad may is remembered, the product or brand is almost always easily recalled.
(False; Challenging; p. 205)

19) A rational appeal is closely tied to the stages of visual and verbal imagining, from cognitive to conative.
(False; Challenging; pp. 215-216)

20) Emotional appeals are not useful for business-to-business advertisements because they do not incorporate cognitive elements.
(False; Challenging; pp. 217-218)

Multiple-Choice Questions

21) The use of white space in an ad may be _____ .
    a) a unique method for overcoming clutter
    b) rejected by most magazine publishers
    c) similar to a "cluttered" ad, in terms of attracting attention
    d) the opposite of a mostly subliminal ad
(a; Easy; pp. 192-193)

22) In the hierarchy of effects model, the last step before the purchase is _____ .
    a) awareness
    b) liking
    c) preference
    d) conviction
(d; Easy; p. 195)

23) Usually, the first step in a purchase decision in the hierarchy of effects model is _____ .
   a) awareness
   b) liking
   c) preference
   d) conviction
   (a; Easy; p. 195)

24) The sequence which matches the typical steps in the hierarchy of effects model is _____ .
   a) cognitive-affective-conative
   b) affective-conative-cognitive
   c) liking-decision-discovery
   d) discovery-liking-decision
   (a; Easy; p. 196)

25) Which emphasizes leverage points and executional frameworks?
   a) hierarchy of effects
   b) MECCAS
   c) visual and verbal cues
   d) conative and cognitive models
   (b; Easy; p. 197)

26) Which is the most easily remembered?
   a) visual cues
   b) verbal cues
   c) peripheral cues
   d) secondary cues
   (a; Easy; p. 199)

27) Visual elements are stored in the brain as _____ .
   a) forms of verbal cues
   b) forms of concentration
   c) degrees of liking
   d) pictures and words
   (d; Easy; p. 199)

28) Visual esperanto is _____ .
   a) an application of the hierarchy of effects model
   b) a universal language for global advertising
   c) a technique for Spanish-speaking advertisers and consumers
   d) the application of a rational leverage point
   (b; Easy; p. 200)

29) Fear advertisements must present _____ .
    a) logic and reason
    b) emotion and reason
    c) severity and vulnerability
    d) degrees of involvement
(c; Easy; p. 202)

30) Which level of fear is most likely to succeed in an advertisement?
    a) a low, non-threatening level
    b) a moderate level
    c) high levels
    d) it's not the level of fear that matters, it's the type
(b; Easy; p. 203)

31) The goal of a humorous ad is to have consumers _____ .
    a) think, remember, laugh
    b) watch, laugh, remember
    c) recall the ad with cued prompts
    d) recall with unaided prompts
(b; Easy; p. 204)

32) Which type of humor is most likely to fail with older consumers?
    a) slapstick
    b) puns and word play
    c) visual gags
    d) sarcasm
(d; Easy; p. 205)

33) Using a female wearing a bikini in advertisement of tools is an example of _____ .
    a) a subliminal sexual cue
    b) decorative model
    c) overt sexuality
    d) sexual suggestiveness
(b; Easy; p. 209)

34) Subliminal sexual messages are _____ .
    a) often ignored by consumers paying little attention to the ad
    b) highly effective with elderly viewers who watch ads more carefully
    c) increasingly used instead of humor
    d) used to advertise children's products
(a; Easy; p. 206)

35) Controversial sexual ads are likely to _____ .
   a) fail to transmit key information
   b) attract attention
   c) be viewed as interesting
   d) contain rational tactics
(a; Easy; p. 209)

36) Decorative models are people who _____ .
   a) are key product spokespersons
   b) are nude models in television ads
   c) adorn a product as a sexual stimulus
   d) design attractive products
(c; Easy; p. 209)

37) "Regular person" models are being used by companies like Wal-Mart in response to _____ .
   a) fear advertising tactics
   b) rational advertising tactics
   c) criticisms about young, thin models being used in clothing ads
   d) not enough men in sexually-oriented advertisements
(c; Easy; pp. 211-212)

38) Using a popular song in an advertisement _____ .
   a) does not have as much of an effect as writing a new tune
   b) transfers the emotional affinity for the song to the product
   c) creates brand parity
   d) causes the product name to be forgotten
(b; Easy; p. 213)

39) Rational appeals _____ .
   a) match the traditional steps of the hierarchy of effects model
   b) often include some sexual content
   c) are focused on image rather than product benefits
   d) are least successful in business-to-business ads
(a; Easy; p. 215)

40) Rational appeals _____ .
   a) are best combined with sexually suggestive ads
   b) rely heavily on quality music to be successful
   c) are most effective when viewers are highly involved and willing to pay attention
   d) are often presented with a decorative model to draw interest to the logic
(c; Easy; p. 216)

41) Emotional appeals _____ .
    a) have been used more frequently in business-to-business ads in the past decade
    b) are designed to evoke cognitive responses
    c) primarily describe product attributes
    d) are difficult to create on television
(a; Easy; p. 217)

42) Scarcity appeals _____ .
    a) only work in children's advertising because adults are aware of the ploy
    b) do not work for children because they cannot process the information
    c) urge consumers to buy a product because of some kind of limitation
    d) urge consumers to save money to buy a product later
(c; Easy; p. 218)

43) For print ads, the most crucial element is the _____ .
    a) headline
    b) proof of claim
    c) amplification
    d) unique selling proposition
(a; Easy; p. 219)

44) The hierarchy of effects model _____ .
    a) only works in the correct sequence
    b) is designed to build recall more than an actual purchase decision
    c) clarifies the advertising approach to use by showing what to stress
    d) leads to impulse buying decisions
(c; Moderate; pp. 195-196)

45) The cognitive component of attitude matches the hierarchy of effects' components of _____ .
    a) awareness and knowledge
    b) liking and preference
    c) conviction and action
    d) the actual purchase
(a; Moderate; p. 196)

46) The affective component of attitude matches the hierarchy of effects' components of _____ .
    a) awareness and knowledge
    b) liking, preference, and conviction
    c) conviction and action
    d) the actual purchase
(b; Moderate; p. 196)

47) The conative component of attitude matches the hierarchy of effects' element of _____ .
   a) knowledge
   b) preference
   c) conviction
   d) the actual purchase
   (d; Moderate; p. 196)

48) A leverage point is the feature of the ad that leads the viewer to transform _____ .
   a) liking for the product to conviction to purchase
   b) the advertising message into a personal value
   c) the visual element into both a mental picture and words
   d) the ad's visual element into affective feelings
   (b; Moderate; p. 198)

49) A verbally-based ad is normally processed _____ .
   a) with little consideration of content
   b) using the central route of the ELM
   c) using the peripheral route of the ELM
   d)
   e) in a hedonic framework
   (b; Moderate; p. 199)

50) Which is an example of visual esperanto?
   a) showing a shared family moment
   b) using a decorative model
   c) tailoring ad copy to a particular region
   d) showing the Rocky Mountains
   (a; Moderate; p. 200)

51) In the behavioral response model, the advertiser emphasizing fear must incorporate into their ad an element of _____ .
   a) deprivation
   b) scarcity
   c) severity
   d) response efficacy
   (c; Moderate; p. 202)

52) In a fear appeal, showing the potential for a devastating injury when seat belts are not used is an example of _____ .
   a) cognition
   b) severity
   c) vulnerability
   d) self-efficacy
   (b; Moderate; p. 202)

53) Humor overcomes clutter by _____ .
   a) making the person laugh
   b) frequently repeating the company's name
   c) capturing attention
   d) making other products less memorable
(c; Moderate; p. 204)

54) Research indicates that humor will _____ .
   a) get a person's attention, but adversely affects the recall of the product's benefits
   b) get a person's attention, but interferes with brand recall
   c) cut through clutter if the humor is tied closely to the product's attributes
   d) elevate a person's mood, which will then be transferred to the product being advertised
(d; Moderate; pp. 204-205)

55) A nude male on a calendar for household furniture is _____ .
   a) a source or spokesperson
   b) a decorative model
   c) an example of subliminal advertising
   d) an example of overt sexuality
(b; Moderate; p. 209)

56) Sensuality in advertising _____ .
   a) requires both visual and verbal cues
   b) requires viewer imagination
   c) is based on subliminal cues
   d) works only with female viewers since they are more romantic then men
(b; Moderate; p. 208)

57) Using songs from popular musicians is _____ .
   a) popular due to low fees for songs because singers seek greater exposure
   b) popular because the affinity for the song transfers to the product
   c) not popular because the songs overwhelm the message
   d) not popular because people remember the musician, not the message
(b; Moderate; p. 213)

58) Rational appeals work best when _____ .
   a) there is low involvement and the product is simple
   b) there is high involvement, but no emotion
   c) there is high involvement and the viewer is willing to pay attention to the ad
   d) they are related more to the product than the amount of involvement
(c; Moderate; p. 216)

59) Emotional appeals are popular because _____ .
   a) they are better at getting a viewer's attention than humor or sexuality
   b) rational appeals are often ignored
   c) they emphasize product features
   d) they often contain subliminal messages
(b; Moderate; p. 216)

60) Which product best fits a scarcity appeal?
   a) televisions
   b) black dress socks
   c) deodorant
   d) a musical compilation CD from one artist
(d; Moderate; p. 218)

61) The amplification of an ad often contains _____ .
   a) imagery or an attention-getting device
   b) allegory or alliteration for memory
   c) a unique selling proposition
   d) an alternative perspective
(c; Moderate; p. 219)

62) A consumer who sees a humorous ad for the first time is in which stage of the Hierarchy of Effects model?
   a) awareness
   b) preference
   c) liking
   d) could be in any of the stages
(d; Challenging; pp. 195-196)

63) In the business-to-business advertisement for Service Metrics, where the man is blindfolded and about ready to step into a manhole, the manhole represents the _____ .
   a) leverage point
   b) appeal
   c) executional framework
   d) personal value
(b; Challenging; p. 198)

64) In the business-to-business advertisement for Service Metrics where the man is blindfolded and about ready to step into a manhole, the manhole illustrates which component of the behavioral response model?
   a) severity
   b) vulnerability
   c) response cost
   d) negative consequence
(b; Challenging; p. 202)

65) In terms of the visual element of an advertisement, an abstract image _____ .
    a) has a higher level of recall than a concrete image
    b) has a lower level of recall than a concrete image
    c) has a greater impact on the affective component of attitude than a concrete image
    d) has a greater impact on the cognitive component of attitude than on the affective component
(b; Challenging, p. 199)

66) Which is an example of visual esperanto?
    a) a photo of a Saturn automobile
    b) a child enjoying an ice cream treat
    c) a description of an office machine
    d) a decorative model
(b; Challenging; p. 200)

67) A successful fear ad creates _____ .
    a) a high level of severity
    b) a high level of response cost
    c) a sense of vulnerability
    d) a response efficacy
(c; Challenging; p. 202)

68) While advertisements in the United States contain more visual sexual themes now than in the past, verbal references to sex _____ .
    a) has actually decreased
    b) has also increased
    c) has taken more of a sensual approach rather than overt sexuality
    has more humor approaches(a; Challenging; p. 206)

69) Clairol's "yes, yes, yes!" campaign is an example of _____ .
    a) overt sexuality
    b) subliminal sexuality
    c) sexual suggestiveness
    d) sensuality
(c; Challenging; p. 207)

70) The types of sexually-oriented ads that will produce the highest level of physiological responses are _____ .
    a) nudity and overt sexuality
    b) nudity and sexual suggestiveness
    c) sensuality and sexual suggestiveness
    d) nudity and partial nudity
(a; Challenging; p. 209)

71) A description of how a search engine can help the web specialist at an e-business feel good about its website's ability to handle the e-commerce traffic is an example of an advertisement using a(n) _____ .
   a) rational appeal
   b) emotional appeal
   c) scarcity appeal
   d) fear appeal
(b; Challenging; pp. 216-217)

72) In England, musicians are _____ .
   a) more likely to agree to let their songs be part of ads than in the U.S.
   b) less likely to agree to let their songs be part of ads than in the U.S.
   c) equally inclined to agree to let their songs be part of ads
   d) banned by law from using songs as ads
(a; Challenging; p. 214)

73) Business-to-business ads have tended to use the rational approach almost exclusively. In recent years, there has been a move to use more _____ .
   a) sex appeals
   b) emotional appeals
   c) fear appeals
   d) scarcity appeals
(b; Challenging; pp. 217-218)

74) The Good Housekeeping seal of approval represents which part of an ad?
   a) the promise of a benefit
   b) amplification
   c) spelling out the benefit or promise
   d) the proof of the claim
(d; Challenging, p. 219)

75) In the advertisement by Curves for Women, consumers are encouraged to "join now" by offering them the rest of the summer free. This portion of the ad corresponds to which step in the hierarchy of effects model?
   a) awareness
   b) knowledge
   c) conviction
   d) the actual purchase
(d; Challenging; pp. 195-196)

76) In the Means-End chain for milk, the calcium content of milk leads to healthier bones, which leads to a display of wisdom and a comfortable life free of osteoporosis. The healthier bones' component of the Means-End chain is the _____ .
   a) product attribute
   b) consumer benefit
   c) leverage point
   d) personal value
(b; Challenging; pp. 197-198)

77) In terms of a fear approach, one reason teenagers who smoke do not quit is because they are afraid they will lose their friends. The social aspect of their lives is more important than the health aspects. In their minds, losing their friends is which component of the behavioral response model?
   a) intrinsic reward
   b) severity
   c) vulnerability
   d) response cost
(d; Challenging; pp. 202-203)

78) All of the following statements about the use of decorative models is true except _____ .
   a) the presence of a decorative model improves ad recognition, but not brand recogniton
   b) attractive models produce higher levels of attention than do less attractive models
   c) the presence of an attractive model produces higher purchase intentions
   d) the presence of a decorative model influences the affective component of attitude
(c; Challenging; pp. 209-210)

79) The Puerto Rico Tourism Company found that the best appeal for vacation destinations is _____ .
   a) rational appeal
   b) emotional appeal
   c) fear appeal
   d) sex appeal
(b; Challenging; p. 216)

80) A television ad that uses a lesbian or gay theme of two individuals meeting for a date would be an example of a(n) _____ .
   a) subliminal sexual approach
   b) sexual suggestiveness approach
   c) sensuality approach
   d) overt sexual approach
(b; Challenging; pp. 207-208)

Short-Answer Questions

81)   How are visual elements of ads stored in the brain?

As both pictures and words.
(Easy; p. 199)

82)   In the behavioral response model, what two elements should a fear ad contain?

1. scarcity
2. vulnerability
(Easy; p. 202)

83)   Describe the sequence that occurs when a humorous ad is successful.

1) The consumer watches, 2) laughs, and 3) most important, remembers. 4) The consumer also attaches positive feelings to the product.
(Easy; p. 204)

84)   Name the components of the hierarchy of effects' model.

- Awareness
- Knowledge
- Liking
- Preference
- Conviction
- The actual purchase

(Moderate; p. 195)

85)   Name the components of the MECCAS model. What does MECCAS stand for?

1. Product attributes
2. Consumer benefits
3. Leverage points
4. Personal values
5. Executional framework

Means-Ends Conceptualization of Components for Advertising Strategy
(Moderate; p. 197)

86) What approaches to sexuality are used in advertising?

- Subliminal techniques
- Nudity or partial nudity
- Sexual suggestiveness
- Overt sexuality
- Sensuality

(Moderate; p. 206)

87) What are the major criticisms of sexuality in advertising?

They are too overt and offensive.
They overemphasize body image.
They create attention, but do not transmit information.
(Moderate; pp. 211-212)

88) What is a scarcity ad? How is scarcity created?

A scarcity ad urges consumers to buy a product because of a limitation. They can be limited-production runs, time restrictions where products are only offered during one part of the year, or a result of deprivation, such as in the "Got Milk" campaign.
(Moderate; p. 218)

89) What roles can music play in advertisements?

- Incidental background
- Primary theme in the ad
- Inspire emotion
- Create favorable reactions to the ad

(Challenging; pp. 212-214)

90) What are the various types of appeals that can be used in advertising and what is the primary benefit of each type?

- Fear – Increases a viewer's interest in an ad as well as recall.
- Humor – Excellent at breaking through ad clutter and getting a viewer's attention.
- Sex – Good at breaking through clutter and increasing a positive attitude toward the brand being advertised, if it is appropriate to a sexual approach.
- Music – Good at capturing attention and linking the ad to emotional feelings.
- Rational – Good for high involvement and complex products.
- Emotions – Excellent for developing the affective component of attitude and developing feelings towards a brand.
- Scarcity – Useful for marketing a product that is in limited supply or available for only a limited amount of time.

(Challenging; pp. 201-218)

CHAPTER 8
ADVERTISING DESIGN
MESSAGE STRATEGIES AND EXECUTIONAL FRAMEWORKS

True-False Questions

1)   A generic message is a direct promotion of a good or service without any claim of superiority.
       (True; Easy; p. 231)

2)   A preemptive message is designed to display a product in comparison to the competition.
       (False; Easy; p. 232)

3)   Negative comparison ads may transfer negative feelings toward the sponsor's product.
       (True; Easy; p. 233)

4)   Demonstration ads are suited to television because the actual product features can be clearly shown.
       (True; Easy; p. 243)

5)   A dead-person endorsement is illegal in most states.
       (False; Easy; p. 246)

6)   Repeating a tag line is ineffective in advertising because the consumer becomes tired of hearing the phrase.
       (False; Easy; p. 252)

7)   Advertisers should avoid simplicity in advertising because it insults the viewer or consumer.
       (False; Easy; p. 253)

8)   The tag line "soup is good food" is an example of hyperbole in advertising.
       (False; Moderate; pp. 231-232)

9)   Affective message strategies are designed to invoke rational decisions, which lead to comparisons and purchases.
       (False; Moderate; p.234)

10)   Impulse buys are linked to conative message strategies.
       (True; Moderate; pp. 235-236)

11)   A slice-of-life ad utilizes celebrity spokespersons offering expert endorsements.
       (False; Moderate; pp. 239-240)

12) Authoritative ads either provide scientific evidence or use an authoritative voice to present the information.
(True; Moderate; p. 242)

13) Typical person sources are not ordinarily credible.
(False; Moderate; p. 247)

14) A celebrity who endorses several products is building credibility as a spokesperson.
(False; Moderate; p. 249)

15) A brand user strategy is a form of comparative strategy.
(False; Challenging; p. 236)

16) Animation is a type of slice-of-life advertising execution.
(False; Challenging; p. 238)

17) Testimonials are an effective executional framework for advertising services.
(True; Challenging; p. 241)

18) Consumer reports and the Good Housekeeping seal of approval are examples of an informative executional framework.
(False; Challenging; p. 242)

19) The principle of campaign duration suggests that all advertisements should be easily recalled by viewers, but without them becoming boring or uninteresting.
(True; Challenging; p. 252)

20) Wal-Mart's emphasis on low prices violates the principle of consistent positioning, which stresses quality instead.
(False; Challenging; p. 252)

Multiple-Choice Questions

21) The original Viagra advertisements were designed to create _____ .
    a) immediate purchases of the product
    b) brand awareness
    c) linkage of the brand name to the corporation's name (Pfizer)
    d) barriers to entry for competing products
(b; Easy; pp. 229-230)

22) Which is <u>not</u> a cognitive message strategy?
  a) generic
  b) preemptive
  c) action-inducing
  d) hyperbole
(c; Easy; p. 231)

23) Which message strategy is most linked with reasoning processes?
  a) cognitive message strategies
  b) brand message strategies
  c) affective message strategies
  d) resonance message strategies
(a; Easy; p. 231)

24) Which cognitive message strategy is a direct promotion of a brand without any claim of superiority?
  a) generic
  b) hyperbole
  c) preemptive
  d) brand
(a; Easy; p. 231)

25) Which is <u>not</u> a type of brand message strategy?
  a) comparative
  b) brand image
  c) brand usage
  d) corporate
(a; Easy; p. 236)

26) Which message strategy is most linked to emotions?
  a) cognitive message strategies
  b) affective message strategies
  c) comparative executional frameworks
  d) unique selling proposition executional frameworks
(b; Easy; p. 234)

27) Which message strategy is most linked to action?
  a) generic message strategies
  b) conative message strategies
  c) corporate brand strategies
  d) affective message strategies
(b; Easy; pp. 235-236)

28) Using music to build emotions surrounding a product is tied to which form of message strategy?
   a) cognitive
   b) affective
   c) brand
   d) conative
   (b; Easy; pp. 234-235)

29) Which message strategy approach stresses the actual product the least?
   a) generic
   b) comparative
   c) hyperbole
   d) corporate
   (d; Easy; p. 237)

30) The Pillsbury Dough Boy is an example of which type of executional framework?
   a) animation
   b) dramatization
   c) testimonial
   d) fantasy
   (a; Easy; p. 239)

31) When a product solves an everyday life problem, the executional framework being used in the ad is most likely to be _____ .
   a) slice-of-life
   b) authoritative
   c) fantasy
   d) informative
   (a; Easy; pp. 239-240)

32) In terms of executional frameworks, a dramatization is similar to, but a more powerful form of story than _____ .
   a) animation
   b) slice-of-life
   c) fantasy
   d) authoritative
   (b; Easy; p. 241)

33) Showing how a product works is which type of executional framework?
   a) slice-of-life
   b) testimonial
   c) demonstration
   d) fantasy
   (c; Easy; p. 242)

34) In terms of an executional framework, showing someone enjoying an exotic experience is a _____ .
   a) testimonial executional framework
   b) dramatization executional framework
   c) slice-of-life executional framework
   d) fantasy executional framework
(d; Easy; p. 243)

35) The key to a testimonial executional framework is _____ .
   a) likeability
   b) negative likeability
   c) credibility
   d) visual consistency
(c; Easy; p. 241)

36) A physician endorsing a specific brand of medicine would have a high level of _____ .
   a) attractiveness
   b) likeability
   c) expertise
   d) personality
(c; Easy; p. 248)

37) When an accountant serves as a spokesperson in an advertisement for an accounting service, receivers who are also accountants find the ad to be more credible based on _____ .
   a) attractiveness
   b) similarity
   c) likeability
   d) persuasiveness
(b; Moderate; p. 247)

38) Wishing to think and act rich, like the spokesperson in an advertisement, is a form of _____ .
   a) empathy
   b) intent to purchase
   c) identification
   d) attractiveness
(c; Moderate; p. 247)

39) A professional athlete endorsing a pain reliever demonstrates _____ .
   a) physical attractiveness
   b) personality
   c) a typical person approach
   d) credibility
(d; Moderate; p. 248)

40)   When Crest claims to be the "cavity fighter," competitors can't make the same claim. This is which type of approach?
        a) generic
        b) preemptive
        c) hyperbole
        d) comparative
    (b; Moderate; p. 232)

41)   A unique selling proposition differs from a preemptive generic approach, because the claim is _____ .
        a) preemptive
        b) testable
        c) emotional
        d) comparative
    (b; Moderate; p. 232)

42)   "Our product is better than brand X" is a form of _____ .
        a) conative message strategy
        b) slice-of-life execution
        c) comparative message strategy
        d) expert authority execution
    (c; Moderate; p. 232)

43)   "The Few. The Proud. The Marines" used in every Marine ad demonstrates _____ .
        a) an identifiable selling point
        b) credibility
        c) campaign duration
        d) repeated tagline
    (d; Easy; pp. 251-253)

44)   The message strategy designed to get viewers to recall memories and emotions is an example of a _____ .
        a) generic message strategy
        b) cognitive message strategy
        c) resonance message strategy
        d) brand user strategy
    (c; Moderate; p. 234)

45)   Which type of message strategies is designed to trigger impulse buys?
        a) unique selling propositions
        b) brand strategies
        c) affective strategies
        d) conative strategies
    (d; Moderate; pp. 235-236)

46) Brand user strategies focus on _____ .
   a) people who use the product
   b) image and loyalty
   c) various uses of the product
   d) emotions and likeability
(a; Moderate; p. 236)

47) Brand usage messages focus on _____ .
   a) favorable comparisons to other products
   b) recall based on emotions
   c) corporate images
   d) product features and uses
(d; Moderate; p. 237)

48) The four components of a slice-of-life format do not include _____ .
   a) encounter
   b) problem
   c) testimonial
   d) solution
(d; Moderate; p. 240)

49) A dramatization execution has a more intense story format than _____ .
   a) a slice-of-life
   b) a testimonial
   c) resonance advertising
   d) conative advertising
(a; Moderate; p. 241)

50) To emphasize credibility, testimonial executions should utilize _____ .
   a) celebrity endorsers
   b) animation
   c) typical persons
   d) negatively likeability against the comparison product
(c; Moderate; p. 241)

51) Authoritative executional frameworks suggest buyers will be influenced by _____ .
   a) brand parity
   b) action-inducing ad properties
   c) rational thought
   d) emotions
(c; Moderate; p. 242)

52) Fantasy approaches rely on _____ .
   a) raw sex and nudity
   b) comparisons of product features
   c) suggestiveness
   d) cognitive thought processes
   (c; Moderate; p. 243)

53) Ads using an informative executional framework are best suited for _____ .
   a) conative message strategies
   b) high involvement purchase decisions
   c) slice-of-life executions
   d) brand image message strategies
   (b; Moderate; pp. 243-244)

54) An ad that is targeted toward stay-at-home wives, which begins with this phrase, "Since I stopped working, I have more time for my kids," is emphasizing _____ .
   a) likeability
   b) similarity
   c) consistency
   d) continuity
   (b; Moderate; p. 247)

55) Giving to a charity because the spokesperson in the ad is a Republican, and the viewer is also a Republican, is based on _____ .
   a) likeability
   b) identification
   c) consistency
   d) empathy
   (b; Moderate; p. 247)

56) Which has the most credibility?
   a) unpaid celebrity spokesperson for a charity
   b) dead-person endorsements
   c) CEOs selling a product
   d) a voice-over by a celebrity
   (a; Moderate; p. 246)

57) Attractiveness consists of physical properties and _____ .
   a) trustworthiness
   b) credibility
   c) personality
   d) expertise
   (c; Moderate; p. 247)

58) A celebrity who endorses several products may suffer decreased _____ .
   a) credibility
   b) likeability
   c) expertise
   d) attractiveness
   (a; Moderate; p. 249)

59) Credibility is an issue when the endorser is <u>not</u> _____ .
   a) likable
   b) believable
   c) consistent
   d) recognizable
   (b; Moderate; p. 248)

60) Typical person ads are difficult because _____ .
   a) the individuals are often perceived as not being credible
   b) do not have a high level of expertise
   c) they are not professional actors so they are more difficult to work with
   d) they are not physically attractive
   (c; Moderate; p. 250)

61) A unique selling proposition message strategy is designed to reduce _____ .
   a) brand parity
   b) recall of competitive products
   c) favorable ratings of competitive products
   d) lost sales due to impulse buys
   (a; Challenging; p. 232)

62) Puffery is most associated with _____ .
   a) generic claims
   b) preemptive messages
   c) hyperbole
   d) comparisons
   (c; Challenging; p. 232)

63) Showing greasy potato chips versus Pringles is an example of _____ .
   a) a preemptive claim of superiority
   b) a generic demonstration of product quality
   c) a negative comparison ad
   d) fighting brand parity through comparison
   (c; Challenging; p. 233)

64) An advertisement that features the work of DuPont to protect the environment is an example of a _____ .
   a) cognitive message strategy
   b) resonance advertising
   c) brand image strategy
   d) corporate message strategy
(d; Challenging; p. 237)

65) Rescuing a boring party by playing a new game is an example of a(n)_____ .
   a) slice-of-life execution
   b) testimonial execution
   c) fantasy execution
   d) informative execution
(a; Challenging; pp. 239-240)

66) Showing how Windex makes a dirty window sparkle is a(n) _____ .
   a) dramatization execution
   b) testimonial execution
   c) demonstration execution
   d) informative execution
(c; Challenging; p. 242)

67) Services being recommended by satisfied customers is a form of _____ .
   a) dramatization execution
   b) testimonial execution
   c) authoritative execution
   d) informative execution
(b; Challenging; p. 241)

68) Rotoscoping is used in a(n)_____ .
   a) animation executional framework
   b) dramatization executional framework
   c) testimonial executional framework
   d) authoritative executional framework
(a; Challenging; p. 239)

69) Ads using the authoritative executional framework utilize _____ .
   a) feelings of resonance
   b) the central route of persuasion of the ELM
   c) the peripheral route of persuasion of the ELM
   d) conative assessments
(b; Challenging; p. 242)

70) Clairol's "yes, yes, yes" ads are an example of _____ .
    a) resonance advertising
    b) action inducing advertising
    c) a fantasy executional framework
    d) rotoscoping
(c; Challenging; p.243)

71) A dessert that is promoted as being "sinfully delicious" with a person sitting on a sandy beach is using _____ .
    a) A resonance message strategy
    b) a slice-of-life executional framework
    c) a fantasy executional framework
    d) a hyperbole message strategy
(c; Challenging; p. 243)

72) Which is least likely to be used in business-to-business ads?
    a) conative message strategies
    b) informative executional frameworks
    c) fantasy executional frameworks
    d) celebrity spokespersons
(c; Challenging; p. 243)

73) Which is most likely to have all five source characteristics?
    a) a celebrity
    b) a typical person
    c) an expert
    d) a CEO
(a; Challenging; p. 247)

74) When selling a copier to another business, which source characteristic would be least important?
    a) expertise
    b) attractiveness
    c) credibility
    d) trustworthiness
(b; Challenging; pp. 247-248)

75) CEOs may suffer from a lower level of likeability and _____ .
    a) expertise
    b) credibility
    c) attractiveness
    d) trustworthiness
(c; Challenging; p. 249)

76) In beating ad clutter, repetition can increase brand and ad recall <u>except</u> when _____ .
    a) the ads are put into different media
    b) competing ads are present
    c) a celebrity spokesperson is used
    d) the ad uses a fantasy executional framework
    (b; Challenging; p. 254)

77) Because ad repetition does not always work, advertisers have begun to take advantage of the principle of variability theory. That means brand and ad recall are increased because the ad _____ .
    a) has several identifiable selling points
    b) is seen by consumers in different environments
    c) uses the same tagline in every venue
    d) uses a typical person spokesperson
    (b; Challenging; p. 254)

78) A print advertisement for Jockey underwear uses the picture of a typical grandmother with a testimony from her about the fit and how her granddaughters now wear jockey. This advertisement illustrates a testimonial execution with a(n) _____ .
    a) cognitive message strategy
    b) affective message strategy
    c) conative message strategy
    d) brand message strategy
    (b; Challenging; pp. 234, 250)

79) Procter & Gamble was instrumental in developing and making popular the _____ .
    a) animation executional framework
    b) testimonial executional framework
    c) authoritative executional framework
    d) slice-of-life executional framework
    (d; Challenging; p. 240)

80) Reebok's claim that it is the only shoe that uses DMX technology, which results in a more comfortable shoe, is an example of a(n)_____ .
    a) generic message strategy
    b) preemptive message strategy
    c) unique selling point message strategy
    d) comparative message strategy
    (c; Challenging; p. 232)

Short-Answer Questions

81)   Name the five major forms of cognitive strategies.

1. Generic
2. Preemptive
3. Unique selling proposition
4. Hyperbole
5. Comparative
(Easy; p. 231)

82)   What is the difference between slice-of-life and dramatization?

Dramatization is more intense.
(Easy; p. 241)

83)   What four types of sources or spokespersons can advertisers utilize?

- Celebrities
- CEOs
- Experts
- Typical persons
(Easy; p. 244)

84)   What are the advantages and disadvantages of comparative ads?

The advantages are they capture attention and are remembered.
The disadvantages are they are less believable and can foster negative attitudes.
(Moderate; pp. 233-234)

85)   What are the two types of affective message strategies? Define both.

1. Resonance advertising connects the product with the consumer's experiences in order to build bonds.
2. Emotional advertising ties emotions to product recall and choice.
(Moderate; pp. 234-235)

86)   What are the two types of conative message strategies? Define both.

1. Action-inducing ads lead directly to behaviors, such as impulse buys.
2. Promotional support ads work in combination with other promotional efforts.
(Moderate; pp. 235-236)

87)   Name and describe the four kinds of brand message strategies.

1. Brand user strategies focus on the type of individual that uses a particular brand.
2. Brand image strategies concentrate on developing a brand personality.
3. Brand usage messages stress different uses of the brand or product.
4. Corporate advertising promotes the company's name and image rather than the individual brand.

(Moderate; pp. 236-237)

88)   Name the executional frameworks advertisers can utilize.

- Animation
- Slice-of-life
- Dramatization
- Testimonial
- Authoritative
- Demonstration
- Fantasy
- Informative

(Moderate; p. 238)

89)   Name the ways to present claims in authoritative ads.

- Experts
- Scientific or survey evidence
- Endorsements by independent organizations
- Satisfied customers

(Moderate; p. 242)

90)   What are the principles of effective advertising?

- Visual consistency
- Campaign duration
- Repeated taglines
- Consistent positioning
- Simplicity
- Identifiable selling point

(Challenging; p. 252)

CHAPTER 9
ADVERTISING MEDIA SELECTION

True-False Questions

1) A media strategy is the process of analyzing and choosing media for an advertising and promotions campaign.
   (True; Easy; p. 264)

2) The person who buys space and also negotiates rates, times, and schedules for ads is normally the creative.
   (False; Easy p. 267)

3) Reach is the number of people, households, or businesses in a target market that are exposed to a message at least once.
   (True; Easy; p. 268)

4) CPM measures the length of time an advertisement runs.
   (False; Easy; p. 269)

5) Recency theory suggests a person must see an advertisement three times before it will have an effect, such as being remembered.
   (False; Easy; p. 273)

6) One major advantage to television is the lack of clutter as compared to other media.
   (False; Easy; p. 275)

7) Newspapers are an excellent advertising medium for local companies.
   (True; Easy; p. 286)

8) Frequency and effective frequency are measures of the impact or intensity of a media plan.
   (False; Moderate; p. 269)

9) If 100,000 people are exposed to an advertisement, the total gross impressions are 100,000 regardless of whether the people actually saw the ad or not.
   (True; Moderate; p. 271)

10) An interstitial ad on a Web page has significant intrusion value.
   (True; Moderate; p. 282)

11) Television is more mobile than radio, giving it better reach.
   (False; Moderate; p. 278)

12) One of the key advantages of magazine advertisements is the short lead-time available, allowing the advertiser to react to current events.
(False; Moderate; p. 284)

13) Billboard advertising normally has a very low CPM.
(True; Moderate; p. 280)

14) Regular viewers of Wheel of Fortune offer the opportunity for greater frequency as compared to an advertisement on the Super Bowl.
(True; Challenging; p. 269)

15) A discontinuous plan of advertising for a perfume would include year-round ads with extra ads during Christmas, Valentine's Day, and Mother's Day.
(False; Challenging; p. 270)

16) The three-exposure hypothesis suggests that a buyer who is actively looking for a new CD player would need to evaluate advertisements for three different players before making a choice.
(False; Challenging; p. 272)

17) The Internet is an effective advertising medium for young, well-educated consumers with high incomes.
(True; Challenging; p. 282)

18) Advertising to business-to-business buyers is normally not cost effective, compared to sales calls.
(False; Challenging; pp. 291-293)

19) Many of the goals of business-to-business advertisements are the same as those devoted to consumers.
(True; Challenging; p. 293)

20) Advertising in international markets is largely the same as in domestic markets because media usage habits are so similar in most countries.
(False; Challenging; pp. 293-294)

Multiple-Choice Questions

21) Which individual formulates a plan as to where and when ads should run?
   a) the creative
   b) the media planner
   c) the media buyer
   d) the client
(b; Easy; p. 266)

22) Which individual negotiates rates for space on billboards and in magazines?
   a) the creative
   b) the media planner
   c) the media buyer
   d) the client
(c; Easy; p. 267)

23) Which is the number of people, households, or businesses in a target market who are exposed to a media vehicle or message schedule?
   a) reach
   b) frequency
   c) demographics
   d) impressions
(a; Easy; p.268)

24) CPM stands for _____ .
   a) cost per thousand
   b) cost per million
   c) cost of permission marketing
   d) choice of premium method
(a; Easy; p. 269)

25) If the CPM for National Geographic is $16.44, which means it cost $16.44 to reach _____ .
   a) the selected target audience
   b) one thousand readers
   c) 1644 readers
   d) one million readers
(b; Easy; p. 269)

26) Which form of media schedule maintains some minimal level of advertising at all times, but increases advertising at periodic intervals?
   a) continuous
   b) gross impressions
   c) pulsating
   d) discontinuous
(b; Easy; p. 270)

27) Five advertisements placed in a newspaper during a four-week period with a readership of 10,000 would create how many gross impressions?
   a) 10,000
   b) 40,000
   c) 50,000
   d) gross impressions can't be calculated with the information provided
(c; Easy; p. 271)

28) An advertisement on television will have the biggest impact _____ .
   a) at the beginning of a set of ads
   b) in the middle of a set of ads
   c) during an infomercial
   d) when the ad is 15 seconds rather than 30 or 45
   (a; Easy; p. 276)

29) Which is not an advantage of television advertising?
   a) high reach
   b) high intrusion value
   c) quality creative opportunities
   d) increased recall due to short copy
   (d; Easy; p. 275)

30) Which is not an advantage of radio advertising?
   a) low production costs
   b) flexibility
   c) long exposure time
   d) intimacy
   (c; Easy; p. 278)

31) Of the following, which features the best quality of color in ads?
   a) magazines
   b) newspapers
   c) billboards
   d) color quality is the same for most print media
   (a; Easy; p. 284)

32) Which medium was used heavily by the alcohol and tobacco industries?
   a) newspaper
   b) magazine
   c) radio
   d) billboards
   (d; Easy; pp. 279-280)

33) Which demographic is most likely to see an Internet ad?
   a) young males who are well educated
   b) older females who are rich
   c) older males with lower education
   d) young females with incomes under $50,000
   (a; Easy; p. 282)

34) Which is <u>not</u> an advantage of direct mail?
    a) high intrusion value
    b) direct response programs are available
    c) the person who opens the mail is usually the household's main buyer
    d) the ability to target geographic market segments
(a; Easy; pp. 287-288)

35) When a marketing team looks for unique ways to reach individuals and groups that will cause them to notice a product or company, the technique is known as _____ .
    a) expenditure marketing
    b) marketing management
    c) guerilla marketing
    d) marketing facilitation
(c; Easy; p. 289)

36) When a firm has its product shown in the background of a television program or film, the advertising technique is known as _____ .
    a) practical marketing
    b) showcase marketing
    c) product placement
    d) passive advertising
(c; Easy; p. 289)

37) The greatest expenditures on business-to-business advertising are made for _____ .
    a) newspaper ads
    b) billboard ads
    c) trade magazines
    d) yellow pages' ads
(c: Easy; p. 292)

38) Which is <u>not</u> an advantage of advertising in trade journals by b-to-b companies?
    a) bypasses gatekeepers
    b) reaches key buyers
    c) low clutter
    d) longer exposure over time when reread
(c; Easy; p. 293)

39) Selling stuffed ducks to increase awareness of the AFLAC brand is a form of _____ .
    a) product placement
    b) secondary advertising
    c) merchandising the advertising
    d) advertising maximization
(c; Moderate; p. 263)

40) CPRP is calculated as _____ .
   a) cost of media buy divided by the vehicle's rating
   b) cost of the media buy multiplied by the number of viewers
   c) ratings divided by gross exposures
   d) cost of media buy divided by gross exposures
(a; Moderate; p. 270)

41) Gross impressions are _____ .
   a) total exposures of an audience to an ad
   b) calculated considering the percentage of a total audience who viewed an ad
   c) viewer reactions to the ad
   d) viewer loyalty to the medium
(a; Moderate; p. 271)

42) Frequency is highest in _____ .
   a) six 15-second television spots
   b) one 45-second spot
   c) five 30-second spot
   d) four 15-second spots
(a; Moderate; p. 268)

43) The technique designed to find out the cost of an advertisement's reaching a particular product's target market is called _____ .
   a) effective frequency
   b) target reach
   c) weighted or demographic CPM
   d) cost per rating point
(c; Moderate; p. 270)

44) What is the key factor in recency theory?
   a) total number of exposures to an ad
   b) three exposures to an ad
   c) viewer's age and gender
   d) selective attention processes
(d; Moderate; p. 273)

45) Recency theory states that a member in a buying center about ready to purchase a copier has _____ .
   a) to see at least three ads for copier machines before they are noticed
   b) an intrusion threshold for copier ads
   c) selective attention to copier ads
   d) little attention to any ads until a copier is purchased
(c; Moderate; p. 273)

46) Of the following media, which is least able to target specific markets?
   a) television
   b) radio
   c) magazines
   d) billboards
(d; Moderate; pp. 280-281)

47) Of the following, which allows the most effective form of a one-on-one message by the spokesperson in the ad?
   a) radio
   b) newspaper
   c) magazine
   d) outdoor
(a; Moderate; p. 278)

48) Of the following media, which has the longest life?
   a) television
   b) radio
   c) newspaper
   d) outdoor
(d; Moderate; pp. 279-281)

49) Newspaper advertising is receiving increasing competition from _____ .
   a) television
   b) radio
   c) Internet
   d) billboards
(c; Moderate; p. 287)

50) Internet ads have _____ .
   a) Short-life spans
   b) Long-life spans
   c) little clutter
   d) visual-only capabilities
(a; Moderate; p. 282)

51) Which advertising medium can incorporate smell?
   a) television
   b) magazine
   c) Internet
   d) radio
(b; Moderate; p. 284)

52) Which medium is least able to accommodate a local company at a low cost?
   a) newspaper
   b) radio
   c) television
   d) billboard
   (c; Moderate; p. 277)

53) Direct mail has which advantage?
   a) low clutter
   b) low nuisance value
   c) business-to-business target marketing is possible
   d) low cost
   (c; Moderate; pp. 287-288)

54) The use of Mercedez Benz in the most recent James Bond film is an example of _____ .
   a) dealership marketing
   b) corporate identification
   c) decorative product marketing
   d) product placement
   (d; Moderate; p. 289)

55) Retailers spend the most on _____ .
   a) newspaper ads
   b) radio ads
   c) television ads
   d) billboards
   (a; Moderate; p. 285)

56) Which is least effective for business-to-business advertising?
   a) Internet
   b) billboards
   c) direct mail
   d) trade journals
   (b; Moderate; pp. 291-293)

57) Using non-business media rather than traditional media (e.g. trade journals) may help a company _____ .
   a) build a stronger brand name
   b) reduce overall advertising expenditures
   c) define target markets more clearly
   d) generate prospect names for sales calls
   (a; Moderate; p. 292)

58) Business-to-business advertising is _____ .
    a) mostly in newspapers
    b) mostly spent on television
    c) looking more like consumer ads
    d) easier to create because of gatekeepers' screening ads
(c; Moderate; p. 292)

59) Media buying in international settings is _____ .
    a) similar in every country
    b) mostly performed by full-service agencies
    c) conducted by media buyers in some countries but advertising agencies in others
    d) subject to international law
(c; Moderate; p. 294)

60) The AFLAC duck was able to _____ .
    a) change customer perceptions
    b) build brand awareness
    c) tie-in to other financial services
    d) increase the price charged by the company
(b; Challenging; pp. 262-263)

61) Conducting research that matches the product to the media and the target market is the primary task for _____ .
    a) the creative
    b) the media planner
    c) the media buyer
    d) the client company
(b; Challenging; pp. 266-267)

62) What is the relationship between the size of an ad agency and the price it pays for spots on television or radio?
    a) the bigger the company, the more that will be paid for advertising
    b) the bigger the company, the less that will be paid for advertising
    c) medium-sized companies get the best deal
    d) there is no consistent relationship
(d; Challenging; p. 267)

63) A company seeking to build brand equity through repeated exposures to the same ads is using the concept of high _____ .
    a) frequency
    b) continuity
    c) exposure
    d) reach
(a; Challenging; p. 268)

64) What do ratings measure?
   a) the relative efficiency of a media vehicle in hitting a target market
   b) the percentage of a firm's target market that is exposed to a particular show or medium such as a magazine
   c) the quality of the vehicle relative to its promotional impact
   d) the degree of clutter on a given night
   (b; Challenging; p. 270)

65) A company that manufactures washing machines is most likely to invest in _____ .
   a) a continuous campaign
   b) a discontinuous campaign
   c) a reach campaign
   d) an audio/visual campaign
   (a; Challenging; p. 270)

66) Effective frequency refers to _____ .
   a) the number of times a target audience must see an ad for it to be effective
   b) the percentage of the audience that must see an ad to achieve an objective
   c) the percentage of the audience that has seen the ad three times
   d) the degree of selective attention given by the target audience relative to the objective
   (a; Challenging; p. 272)

67) If effective reach and frequency are too high _____ .
   a) the company needs a larger advertising budget
   b) the company spent all of its advertising budget
   c) some of the company's budget may be wasted on extra exposures
   d) the company may need to choose additional media for future ads
   (c; Challenging; p. 272)

68) The three exposure hypothesis is based on _____ .
   a) intrusion value
   b) repeated exposures to overcome clutter
   c) selective attention
   d) interstitial effects
   (b; Challenging; p. 273)

69) For business-to-business ads, a visual presentation of the speed of a laser printer and its superiority is best suited to _____ .
   a) television
   b) radio
   c) newspaper
   d) trade journal
   (a; Challenging; p. 277)

70)	A rotation program for billboards expands the advertisement's _____ .
  a) reach
  b) target market
  c) variability
  d) pulsating campaign
(a; Challenging; p. 280)

71)	An Internet ad is likely to have _____ .
  a) a long life
  b) low clutter
  c) high attention from a person who clicks on a site
  d) high reach
(c; Challenging; p. 282)

72)	Which normally provides the greatest or longest level of attention?
  a) television
  b) radio
  c) magazine
  d) billboard
(c; Challenging; p. 284)

73)	Seeing a Federal Express sign in the background behind a play at a sports event is a form of _____ .
  a) event marketing
  b) continuous advertising
  c) product placement
  d) merchandising the advertising
(c; Challenging; p. 289)

74)	Seventy-five percent of all business-to-business advertising dollars are spent on _____ .
  a) television
  b) radio
  c) print media
  d) Web site development and advertisements
(c; Challenging; pp. 292-293)

75)	Which statement is true?
  a) Television is the most dominant medium for advertising in all international markets.
  b) Many elite European customers prefers media other than television.
  c) Most ads can simply be translated into a foreign language.
  d) Media buying habits are similar within continents of the world.
(b; Challenging; p. 293)

76) If an advertisement costs $200,000, the number of viewers is 2,000,000, and the rating is 2.0, the cost per rating point (CPRP) is _____ .
   a) $100
   b) $1,000
   c) $10,000
   d) $100,000
(d; Challenging; p. 270)

77) If an advertisement appears on ER three times and ER has a Nielsen rating of 12.3, the gross rating points (GRP) would be_____ .
   a) 4.1
   b) 12.3
   c) 36.9
   d) there is not enough information to calculate the GRP
(c; Challenging; p. 269)

78) If a magazine ad costs $500,000, total readership is 20,000,000, but only 2,000,000 fit the advertiser's target profile, the weighted (or demographic) CPM would be _____ .
   a) $25
   b) $250
   c) $2,500
   d) $10
(b; Challenging; p. 270)

79) The media multiplier effect means _____ .
   a) the combined impact of using two or more media is stronger than using either medium alone
   b) the combined effect of television and magazines will increase recall by at least 25%
   c) the use of both trade journals and consumer journals for business-to-business ads will have a greater impact than using either medium alone
   d) that if three different media or used, the combined impact is greater than if only two different media are used
(a; Challenging; p. 290)

80) In terms of media buying, in Brazil and India, media time is purchased almost entirely by _____ .
   a) full-service advertising agencies
   b) full-service media buying firms
   c) freelance media buying firms
   d) subsidiaries of advertising agencies that specialize in media buys
(a; Challenging; p. 294)

Short-Answer Questions

81)   Describe the roles of the media planner and the media buyer.

The media planner is the individual who formulates the program stating where and when to place advertisements. The media buyer is the person who buys the space, negotiates rates, times, and schedules for the ads.
(Easy; pp. 266-268)

82)   Define reach, frequency, continuity, and gross impressions.

Reach is the number of people, households, or businesses in a target audience exposed to a media vehicle or message schedule at least one time during a given time period. Frequency is the average number of times an individual, household, or business within a target market is exposed to a particular advertisement within a specified time period. Continuity is the schedule or pattern of advertisement placements within an advertising campaign period. Gross Impressions are the number of exposures of the audience to an advertisement.
(Easy; pp. 268-271)

83)   What are the primary benefits of television advertising? The primary problems?

The benefits are: high reach, high frequency potential, low cost per contact, quality creative opportunities, high intrusion value, and segmentation possibilities through cable outlets. The problems are: clutter, channel-surfing during commercials, short amount of copy, high cost per ad, and low recall due to clutter.
(Moderate; p. 275)

84)   What are the primary benefits of radio advertising? The primary problems?

The advantages are: lower cost per spot than television, low production costs, music can match the station's programming, high potential segmentation, flexibility, ability to modify ads to fit local conditions, intimacy with the deejay, creative opportunities, and it is mobile. The disadvantages are: short exposure time, low attention, few chances to reach a national audience, and target duplications when several stations in a region use the same format.
(Moderate; p. 278)

85)   What are the primary benefits of newspaper advertising? The primary problems?

The advantages of newspapers are: they give higher priority to local advertisers, coupon and special response features, high credibility, strong audience interest among readers, longer copy is possible, flexibility, and advertisers receive cumulative volume discounts. The disadvantages are: Internet competition, clutter, short life span, poor quality color, a limited audience (over 25), and some poor purchasing procedures.
(Moderate; p. 286)

86)	What are the primary benefits of magazine advertising? The primary problems?

The advantages of magazines are: high segmentation is possible, the audience is targeted by magazine type, high color quality, the availability of special features such as fold-outs or scratch and sniff, long life, direct response techniques, and they are read during leisure time, giving each ad more attention. The disadvantages are: long lead-time before an ad runs, little flexibility, high cost, high clutter, and declining readership of some magazines. (Moderate; p. 283)

87)	What are the primary benefits of Internet advertising? The primary problems?

The benefits of Internet advertising are: creative possibilities, short lead-time to create an ad, simplicity of segmentation, high audience interest on each Web site, and it is easy to measure responses. The disadvantages are: clutter on each site, it is difficult to place ads and buy time, the ads only reach computer owners, low intrusion value, and it is hard to retain the interest of Web surfers.
(Moderate; p. 281)

88)	What are the primary benefits of outdoor advertising? The primary problems?

The advantages of outdoor advertising are that it is large and spectacular, key geographic areas can be selected, it's accessible for local ads, low cost per impression, broad reach, and high frequency on commuter routes. The disadvantages of billboards are: legal limitations, short exposure time, brief messages, little segmentation is possible, and clutter on highly traveled routes.
(Moderate; p. 280)

89)	Other than media, name five other places in which advertisements may appear.

Possible answers include:
- Direct mail
- Leaflets, brochures, carry-home menus
- Carry-home store bags
- Ads on t-shirts and caps
- Ads on movie trailers (video and in theaters)
- Freestanding road signs
- Motel room ads on ash trays, towels, ice chests, etc.
- Yellow pages and phone books
- Mall kiosks
- Faxed ads
- Ads on video replay scoreboards
- In-house magazines (e.g., airlines)
- Walls of airports, subways, bus terminals, and inside cabs and buses
(Moderate; p. 288)

90)   Name the challenges present in business-to-business media selection and in international media selection.

The challenges in business-to-business advertising include getting past the gatekeeper, selecting proper media, overcoming clutter, creating attention and interest in ads, identifying target markets, and spending ad money wisely. The challenges in international markets include finding out how to properly make media buys, media selection to match local audiences, tailoring ads to local communities, overcoming language and cultural barriers, and making sure ads convey the proper message. (Challenging; pp. 291-295)

CHAPTER 10
TRADE PROMOTIONS

True-False Questions

1) Trade promotions are used by manufacturers and other members of the marketing channel to help push products through to retailers.
   (True; Easy; p. 307)

2) Sales promotions are sent to end-users and customers while trade promotions are not.
   (True; Easy; p. 307)

3) A trade promotion is a physical product sent as part of a promotional deal.
   (False; Easy; p. 307)

4) Forward-buying is purchasing extra inventory while it is on-deal.
   (True; Easy; p. 311)

5) Cooperative advertising takes place when the consumer pays part of the advertising cost.
   (False; Easy; p. 316)

6) POP is short for "Place on Page," an Internet advertising term to designate an ad placement.
   (False; Easy; p. 321)

7) Large manufacturers often have a major advantage in the area of trade promotions, compared to small manufacturers and vendors.
   (True; Easy; p. 329)

8) An off-invoice allowance is money paid to retailers who are willing to bypass wholesalers.
   (False; Moderate; p. 309)

9) Slotting fees are utilized to cut prices on large shipments of goods to a retail chain.
   (False; Moderate; p. 309)

10) Exit fees are routinely paid when a product succeeds and is given a larger amount of shelf space.
    (False; Moderate; p. 310)

11) A Cooperative Merchandising Agreement is formed between two manufacturers seeking to jointly advertise products.
    (False; Moderate; p. 313)

12) A premium or bonus pack offers more merchandise than a price discount.
(True; Moderate; p. 315)

13) A bill-back program is a form of off-invoice allowance, which is then billed later.
(False; Moderate; p. 316)

14) Many large national and international trade shows are losing customers to niche shows.
(True; Moderate; p. 320)

15) A drop-ship allowance makes it possible to bypass wholesalers and brokers.
(True; Challenging; p. 309)

16) A diversion is a form of exit fee where funds are transferred from failing products to successful products.
(False; Challenging; p. 312)

17) Spiff money takes the form of prizes paid to consumers in sales contests.
(False; Challenging; p. 312)

18) Slotting fees are considered almost like extortion because they insist the retailer join in cooperative advertising programs.
(False; Challenging; p. 310)

19) A major concern of trade promotions in the grocery industry is that over 70% of the time manufacturers must offer some type of trade promotion to move their merchandise.
(True; Challenging; p. 329)

20) Brand image is not affected by trade promotions' programs since the programs are not directly connected to advertising.
(False; Challenging; p. 330)

Multiple-Choice Questions

21) What distinguishes trade promotions from other marketing and IMC tools?
   a) They involve extensive advertising.
   b) Retail customers are the primary target of the effort.
   c) They are used to entice other members of the marketing channel to make purchases.
   d) They are limited to activities by manufacturers.
   (c; Easy; p. 307)

22) Which is <u>not</u> a recipient of trade promotions?
   a) end-users and consumers
   b) retailers and distributors
   c) wholesalers
   d) brokers and agents
(a; Easy; p. 307)

23) Offering financial incentives to channel members in order to motivate them to make a purchase is a _____ .
   a) trade allowance
   b) trade incentive
   c) trade contest
   d) vendor support program
(a; Easy; p. 308)

24) Financial discounts on cases of merchandise ordered are called _____ .
   a) consumer promotions
   b) off-invoice allowances
   c) drop-ship allowances
   d) spiff money
(b; Easy; p. 309)

25) Money paid to retailers who are willing to bypass wholesalers, brokers, and distributors when making prepaid orders is _____ .
   a) a consumer promotion
   b) an off-invoice allowance
   c) a drop-ship allowance
   d) an exit fee
(c; Easy; p. 309)

26) Funds paid to retailers to stock new products are known as _____ .
   a) prepaid off-invoice allowances
   b) drop-ship allowances
   c) quantity discounts
   d) slotting fees
(d; Easy; p. 309)

27) Monies paid to remove an item from a retailer's inventory are called _____ .
   a) reverse slotting fees
   b) brokerage allowances
   c) exit fees
   d) cooperative merchandising agreements
(c; Easy; p. 310)

28) When a retailer purchases excess inventory of a product while it is on-deal to sell later when it is off-deal, the process is known as _____ .
   a) a diversion
   b) quantity-seeking
   c) forward buying
   d) a slotting fee
(c; Easy; p. 311)

29) When a retailer purchases a product on-deal in one location and ships it to another where it is off-deal, the process is known as _____ .
   a) exit forwarding
   b) a diversion
   c) a transaction alteration
   d) volume buying
(b; Easy; p. 312)

30) Rewards given to brokers, retail salespeople and stores, and others as prizes for winning a contest are known as _____ .
   a) slotting fees
   b) volume incentives
   c) spiff money
   d) pay for play
(c; Easy; p. 312)

31) A formal agreement between a retailer and a manufacturer to undertake a marketing program is called _____ .
   a) an alliance of capital
   b) a cooperative merchandising agreement
   c) a venture agreement
   d) a sales promotion
(b; Easy; p. 313)

32) Offering free merchandise for placing an order is known as _____ .
   a) a slotting fee
   b) a discount invoice
   c) spiff money
   d) a premium or bonus pack
(d; Easy; p. 315)

33) In most cases, a bill-back program takes place between _____ .
   a) a customer and a retailer
   b) two manufacturers
   c) a manufacturer and a wholesaler
   d) a manufacturer and a retailer
(d; Easy; p. 316)

34) When a manufacturer offers to pay part of the costs of a retail advertising campaign, it is known as _____ .
    a) incentive marketing
    b) target market advertising
    c) cooperative advertising
    d) specialty advertising
(c; Easy; p. 316)

35) In a trade show, a power buyer would be _____ .
    a) retail buyers attending a trade show
    b) a member of upper management or key purchasing agents with the authority to buy
    c) a broker or distributor with a large international organization attending a trade show
    d) an exhibitor attending a trade show
(a; Easy; p. 318)

36) Specialty advertising, such as pens or coffee mugs, are also called _____ .
    a) trade allowances
    b) trade incentives
    c) giveaways
    d) merchandising the advertising
(c; Easy; p.320)

37) When you receive a gift and wish to return a favor, the process is known as _____ .
    a) an approach-avoidance conflict
    b) an obligation
    c) diversion
    d) reciprocation
(d; Easy; p. 321)

38) POP stands for _____ .
    a) Print-offer proposal
    b) publicity over protocol
    c) point of purchase
    d) place of publication
(c; Easy; p. 321)

39) A push strategy focuses on _____ .
    a) consumers making requests for merchandise
    b) retailers being enticed to place a product on store shelves
    c) manufacturers seeking additional advertising dollars
    d) media buyers finding new ways to buy ad space
(b; Easy; p. 326)

40) A contest prize presented to a retail store is _____ .
    a) a trade promotion
    b) a consumer promotion
    c) a cooperative merchandising agreement
    d) specialty advertising
(a; Moderate; p. 307)

41) A wholesaler is most likely to be dissatisfied with a manufacturer's _____ .
    a) off-invoice allowance
    b) drop-ship allowance
    c) slotting fees
    d) exit fees
(b; Moderate; p. 309)

42) A retailer stands to gain a direct payment from _____ .
    a) an off-invoice allowance
    b) a drop-ship allowance
    c) slotting fees
    d) forward buying
(c; Moderate; p. 309)

43) It takes at least a retail operation with multiple outlets to engage in _____ .
    a) slotting fees
    b) exit fees
    c) forward buying
    d) diversions
(d; Moderate; p. 312)

44) Extra shipping costs are incurred when a retailer engages in _____ .
    a) slotting fees
    b) exit fees
    c) forward buying
    d) diversions
(d; Moderate; p. 312)

45) Extra costs for carrying inventory occur when a retailer engages in _____ .
    a) spiff money
    b) exit fees
    c) forward buying
    d) cooperative merchandising agreements
(c; Moderate; p. 311)

46) Buying a full truckload of merchandise occurs with _____ .
   a) a producing plant allowance
   b) a calendar promotional campaign
   c) a corporate sales program
   d) a cooperative merchandising agreement
(a; Moderate; p. 314)

47) The primary difference between a back-haul allowance and a producing plant allowance is in the back-haul allowance, _____ .
   a) the retailer furnishes delivery trucks
   b) the manufacturer furnishes delivery trucks
   c) the distributor furnishes delivery trucks
   d) the costs of shipping are divided equally
(a; Moderate; p. 314)

48) A cross-dock or pedal run allowance means _____ .
   a) several manufacturers ship on one truck
   b) several distributors ship on one truck
   c) a retailer divides a shipment from one truck among several stores
   d) the costs of shipping are prepaid by the distributor
(c; Moderate; p. 315)

49) A bill-back program means _____ .
   a) a manufacturer will bill back a retailer for a vendor support program
   b) a retailer will bill back a manufacturer for a vendor support program
   c) a consumer will bill back a retailer for defective merchandise
   d) a consumer will bill back a manufacturer for defective merchandise
(b; Moderate; p. 316)

50) The "Intel inside" program is a form of _____ .
   a) direct marketing
   b) cooperative advertising
   c) producer markup combined with retailer pass-alongs
   d) manufacturer's prerogative
(b; Moderate; p. 317)

51) Co-op money is often unclaimed for every reason listed below except _____ .
   a) co-op claims are rejected by manufacturers because of filing errors
   b) retailers are unaware of a co-op program
   c) media outlets may reject a proposed ad using a co-op program
   d) purchase accruals are tracked inaccurately by the retailer
(c; Moderate; p. 316)

52) At a trade show, narrowing down contacts to the most promising group is called _____ .
    a) prospecting
    b) finding the power buyer
    c) closing the deal
    d) identifying participants
(a; Moderate; p. 318)

53) Specialty advertising is based on the concept of _____ .
    a) specialization
    b) prospecting
    c) identification
    d) reciprocation
(d; Moderate; p. 321)

54) POPs are based on the concept of _____ .
    a) Pull-demand strategy
    b) brand parity
    c) impulse buys
    d) reciprocation
(c; Moderate; p. 322)

55) Which is not an objective of a trade promotions campaign?
    a) increase initial distribution
    b) identify consumer buying habits
    c) obtain better shelf space
    d) support established brands
(b; Moderate; p. 325)

56) Which is not an objective of a trade promotions campaign?
    a) build retail inventories
    b) identify members of a retail's buying center
    c) reduce excess manufacturer inventory
    d) build wholesale inventories
(b; Moderate; p. 325)

57) A "truckload" sale, where merchandise is sold at a major discount because the retailer making a huge order for goods is probably due to _____ .
    a) a producing plant allowance
    b) an effective sales contest
    c) exit fees paid by the retailer
    d) a cooperative merchandising agreement
(a; Challenging; p. 314)

58) A pallet of automobile batteries, complete with a display shelf, is part of _____ .
   a) a cross promotion
   b) multi-manufacturer marketing
   c) a corporate sales program
   d) a back-haul allowance
(c; Challenging; p. 314)

59) A ready-to-display pallet of goods is used with _____ .
   a) a calendar promotional campaign
   b) a corporate sales program
   c) a cooperative merchandising agreement
   d) prize money from a contest
(b; Moderate; p. 314)

60) A calendar promotion campaign encourages all of the following except _____ .
   a) rotating on-deal brands by a retailer
   b) greater loyalty to the manufacturer's brand on-deal
   c) brand equity
   d) greater store loyalty
(d; Moderate; p. 314)

61) Which is often tied to holiday promotions?
   a) off-invoice discount
   b) slotting fees
   c) exit fees
   d) training programs
(a; Challenging; p. 309)

62) Which is not a justification for slotting fees?
   a) Retailers must invest time and money in new products.
   b) The fees help retailers finalize decisions about carrying new products.
   c) The fees reduce the number of new products that are introduced each year.
   d) The fees level the playing field between small and large retail outlets.
(d; Challenging; pp. 309-310)

63) Exit fees are associated with _____ .
   a) product differentiation
   b) brand parity
   c) product failures
   d) corporate image maintenance
(c; Challenging; p. 310)

64) A calendar promotion may result in a retailer using _____ .
    a) forward buying
    b) slotting fees
    c) exit fees
    d) cooperative advertisements
(a; Challenging; p. 314)

65) Producing plant allowances are typically used by _____ .
    a) large manufacturers
    b) small manufacturers
    c) wholesalers and distributors with large retailers
    d) small retail operations that typically order just one or two pallets of merchandise
(b; Challenging; p. 314)

66) A bonus pack is often associated with _____ .
    a) a minimum order size
    b) reductions in slotting fees charged
    c) forgiving the obligation of an exit fee
    d) producing plant allowance
(a; Challenging; p. 315)

67) The two most frequently utilized vendor support programs are _____ .
    a) POPs and CMAs
    b) bill backs and co-op advertising
    c) premiums and bonus packs
    d) back-haul and producing plant allowances
(b; Challenging; p. 316)

68) Co-op advertising programs often stipulate all but the following _____ .
    a) monies accrued for purchases over time
    b) no competing products can be advertised
    c) the manufacturer's product must be displayed prominently in the ad
    d) retailers must pay the incentive fees
(d; Challenging; p. 316)

69) Which is not a form of specialty advertising?
    a) calendar
    b) contest prize
    c) mug
    d) pen and pencil set
(b; Challenging; pp. 320-321)

70) Which is <u>not</u> associated with a POP?
    a) making an impression as the consumer leaves the store
    b) creating reciprocation
    c) inciting impulse buys
    d) creating tie-ins with other promotional efforts
(b; Challenging; pp. 321-324)

71) Which is <u>not</u> a current trend in POP programs?
    a) larger displays with some type of motion components
    b) greater integration with Web site programs
    c) displays that routinely change messages
    d) increased ability to track results
(a; Challenging; pp. 323-324)

72) A consumer asking for a new magazine to be stocked at a newsstand is an example of what type of strategy?
    a) push strategy
    b) pull strategy
    c) reciprocation strategy
    d) trade allowance strategy
(b; Challenging; p. 326)

73) A cooperative advertising campaign can be associated with _____ .
    a) a successful POP program
    b) demand push
    c) demand pull
    d) prospecting
(b; Challenging; p. 326)

74) When one company's specialty advertising program is undercut by another offering a more valuable item, which goal is affected?
    a) countering competitive actions
    b) building retail inventories
    c) increasing order sizes
    d) reducing manufacturer's inventories
(a; Challenging; p. 326)

75) Offering co-op advertising dollars to retail stores would most likely fulfill which goal?
    a) countering competitive actions
    b) obtaining initial distribution
    c) building retail inventories
    d) enhancing channel relationships
(d; Challenging; p. 327)

76) The buyer at Target for electronic calculators has just received an offer from a large manufacturer of electronic calculators that if Target will purchase 10,000 calculators within the next 30 days, they will receive a 10% discount and the manufacturer will ship them directly from the their plants to Target's warehouses. This is an example of _____ .
   a) an off-invoice allowance
   b) a drop-ship allowance
   c) a cooperative merchandise agreement
   d) a producing plant allowance
(b; Challenging; p. 309)

77) When provided with an offer of a 10% discount to purchase 10,000 electronic calculators within the next 30 days, Target buys 30,000 instead to take advantage of the price discount. Target will offer the calculator to consumers at a discount during the special sale, but then have additional calculators to sell when the sale is over. This is an example of _____ .
   a) an off-invoice allowance
   b) cross-dock or pedal run allowance
   c) forward buying
   d) diversion
(c; Challenging; p. 311)

78) Sony is promoting a special coupon and sale on its stereos. Stores that sell at least 100 stereos during the next 30 days will receive an extra stereo, free, for each 20 they sell over the 100. This is an example of a _____ .
   a) cross-dock or pedal run
   b) calendar promotion
   c) corporate sales program
   d) premium or bonus pack
(d; Challenging; p. 315)

79) Research has indicated all of the ingredients listed below will increase the effectiveness of POP displays except _____ .
   a) brand signs
   b) a tie-in to a trade promotion
   c) a tie-in to a movie, sport or charity
   d) an inflatable component or mobile above the POP display
(b; Challenging; p. 323)

80) All of the following are potential problems associated with trade promotion programs except _____ .
   a) costs
   b) the impact on small manufacturers
   c) over-reliance on trade promotions to move merchandise
   d) inability to tie a trade promotion to a consumer promotion
(b; Challenging; p. 329)

Short-Answer Questions

81) What are the four main types of trade allowances? Describe each one.

1. An off-invoice allowance encourages orders by granting financial discounts.
2. A drop-ship allowance is a discount offered to retailers for bypassing wholesalers and taking direct delivery.
3. Slotting fees are funds paid to retailers to stock new products.
4. Exit fees are monies paid to remove an item from a retailer's inventory.
(Moderate; pp. 308-310)

82) What are the disadvantages of trade allowances?

- Retailers may keep the allowance and not pass it on to retail customers
- Forward buying or purchasing an excess of product when it is on-deal
- Diversions or purchasing product on-deal in one store and shipping it to another where it is not
(Moderate; pp. 311-312)

83) Name various forms of trade contests.

- Brokers versus brokers
- Wholesalers versus wholesalers
- Retail stores within a chain versus each other
- Retail store chain versus other retail chains
- Individual salespersons within retail stores versus each other
(Moderate; p. 312)

84) Name and briefly describe the types of trade incentives that are offered.

Cooperative merchandising agreements are formed between a retailer and a manufacturer to undertake a cooperative marketing effort.
Calendar promotions are campaigns the retailer designs for customers through manufacturer trade incentives.
Corporate sales programs are those offered across a manufacturer's total brand portfolio and are shipped in ready-to-display pallets.
Producing plant allowances are full or half-truck loads of merchandise shipped to one place and granted a major discount.
A back-haul allowance is where the retailer pays the cost of shipping.
A cross-dock or pedal run allowance divides a truckload among retailers in an area.
A premium or bonus back offers additional merchandise rather than price discounts.
(Challenging; pp. 313-315)

85) Name and briefly describe two vendor support programs.

(1) A bill-back program occurs when the manufacturer pays the retailer for a special product display by refunding the money to the retailer that bills back the amount. (2) A cooperative advertising program is where the manufacture and retailer share the costs of advertising.
(Challenging; pp. 316-317)

86) Name and describe the five categories of buyers who attend trade shows.

1. Education seekers who want to browse and learn but not buy.
2. Reinforcement seekers who want reassurances about past purchases.
3. Solution seekers who want problems solved and are in a buying mode.
4. Buying teams who are groups ready to buy.
5. Power buyers, who are members of upper management or key purchasing agents with the authority to buy.
(Challenging; pp. 318-320)

87) When are specialty or niche trade shows most effective?

When the goals of the vendor are (1) to establish a client base quickly, (2) establish a new brand, or (3) to promote a new product.
(Challenging; p. 320)

88) What causes a POP to go unused?

It is inappropriate for the product, does not receive consumer responses, is too seasonal, is poorly built, is the wrong size, or is inappropriate for the channel.
(Challenging; p. 322-323)

89) Name three new trends in POP displays.

1. Integration with Web site programs
2. Displays that routinely change messages
3. There is better tracking of results.
(Challenging; p. 323)

90)   What goals or objectives are associated with trade promotions?

- Better initial distribution
- Obtain prime retail locations or shelf space
- Support established brands
- Counter competitive actions
- Increase order sizes
- Build retail inventories
- Reduce excess manufacturer inventories
- Enhance channel relationships
- Enhance the overall IMC program

(Challenging; pp. 325-328)

CHAPTER 11
CONSUMER PROMOTIONS

True-False Questions

1) Consumer promotions or sales promotions are the incentives aimed at the firm's customers.
   (True; Easy; p. 338)

2) FSI stands for Full Standing Inventory, which means the ad campaign is complete.
   (False; Easy; p. 339)

3) The majority of advertising coupons are distributed through print media.
   (True; Easy; p. 339)

4) Free-in-the-mail premiums are gifts individuals receive for purchasing products.
   (True; Easy; p. 343)

5) The consumer is required to make a purchase when entering a sweepstakes.
   (False; Easy; p. 346)

6) Refunds are paid on soft goods; rebates are paid on hard goods, such as cars or appliances.
   (True; Easy; p. 349)

7) Direct sampling is a program in which samples are given directly to consumers in a retail store.
   (False; Easy; p. 350)

8) Instant redemption coupons are a form of direct sampling.
   (False; Moderate; p. 340)

9) One advantage to the seller is that premiums allow for the full price to be charged for a product.
   (True; Moderate; p. 343)

10) Premiums tend to have long life spans.
    (False; Moderate; p. 344)

11) A contest requires the use of a skill while a sweepstakes relies on random chance.
    (True; Moderate; p. 346)

12) In a contest, an intrinsic value is simply playing the game or participating.
    (True; Moderate; p. 346)

13) Refunds and rebates suffer the disadvantages of cost and paperwork.
(True; Moderate; p. 349)

14) Very few sales promotions are used in business-to-business settings because of the nature of the customers involved.
(False; Moderate; p. 356)

15) Placing a coupon for dip on a bag of potato chips is called a bounce-back coupon approach.
(False; Challenging; p. 340)

16) Premiums are normally much more successful than coupons in increasing sales.
(False; Challenging; p. 343)

17) An effective rebate program is based on visibility and familiarity.
(False; Challenging; pp. 349-350)

18) It is not possible to offer sampling programs over the Internet.
(False; Challenging; p. 351)

19) Price-off programs are more difficult to offer in business-to-business relationships because prices are normally fixed by contract.
(True; Challenging; p. 357)

20) Contests and sweepstakes are highly effective in the U.S., but not in other countries due to cultural differences.
(False; Challenging; p. 359)

Multiple-Choice Questions

21) The two most general categories of promotions are consumer franchise-building promotions and consumer _____ .
   a) price-incentive promotions
   b) nonfranchise-building promotions
   c) sales-building promotions
   d) sales promotions
(b; Easy; p. 338)

22) Free Standing Inserts are found in _____ .
   a) magazines
   b) newspapers
   c) shopping malls
   d) catalogs
(b; Easy; p. 339)

23) A coupon placed on a package to be used during the purchase is called a _____ .
   a) Free-standing coupon
   b) Bounce-back coupon
   c) Instant-redemption coupon
   d) rebate coupon
   (c; Easy; p. 340)

24) When a cash register triggers a coupon for a competitor's product, it is called a _____ .
   a) Bounce-back coupon
   b) scanner-delivered coupon
   c) cross-ruff coupon
   d) response offer coupon
   (b; Easy; p. 340)

25) A coupon on a bottle of Pepsi, offering a deal on a bag of potato chips, is called _____ .
   a) cross-ruff coupon
   b) scanner-delivered coupon
   c) response-offer coupon
   d) instant-redemption coupon
   (a; Easy; p. 340)

26) An Internet request, 1-800, or 1-888 numbers that lead to the issuance of a coupon is called _____ .
   a) bounce-back
   b) scanner delivered
   c) instant redemption
   d) response offer
   (d; Easy; p. 341)

27) The typical response for a coupon distribution is _____ .
   a) about 2%
   b) about 10%
   c) about 20%
   d) over 30%
   (a; Easy; p. 341)

28) Coupon fraud or redeeming unused coupons is called _____ .
   a) misredemption
   b) counterfeiting
   c) mass cutting
   d) back billing
   (c; Easy; p. 342)

29) A gift sent by mail to a customer, based on a proof-of-purchase receipt, is called _____ .
    a) free-in-the-mail
    b) self-liquidating
    c) proof by mail
    d) a revolving premium
(a; Easy; p. 343)

30) A "write our new slogan" event that awards a prize to the winning slogan is _____ .
    a) A contest
    b) A sweepstakes
    c) A premium
    d) illegal in most states
(a; Easy; p. 346)

31) For most people, a free trip to Hawaii is an example of a prize with high _____ .
    a) intrinsic value
    b) extrinsic value
    c) redemption rates
    d) Internet inquiries
(b; Easy; p. 346)

32) A cash award for purchasing an automobile is _____ .
    a) a refund
    b) a rebate
    c) a price-off
    d) an instant redemption
(b; Easy; p. 349)

33) Providing a small sample of laundry detergent with the purchase of dryer sheets is called _____ .
    a) direct sampling
    b) response sampling
    c) cross-ruff sampling
    d) media sampling
(a; Easy; p. 351)

34) Samples distributed at a site, such as a state fair, parade, or sporting event, is called _____ .
    a) direct sampling
    b) response sampling
    c) media sampling
    d) selective sampling
(d; Easy; p. 351)

35) Adding an extra bar of soap to a three pack is called _____ .
    a) a rebate pack
    b) a prize package
    c) a bonus pack
    d) a selective sample
    (c; Easy; p. 352)

36) When two products from the same company are promoted together, using one consumer promotion, it is called _____ .
    a) an intracompany tie-in
    b) an intercompany tie-in
    c) an overlay
    d) a premium
    (a; Easy; p. 355)

37) When a manufacturer offers a special promotion to other companies for their use and not for resale, it is a _____ .
    a) consumer promotion
    b) bonus program
    c) trade promotion
    d) brand awareness program
    (a; Easy; p. 356)

38) An organization creating an international consumer promotions program should utilize _____ .
    a) a cultural assimilator
    b) a governmental regulator
    c) a management expert
    d) a tactics manager
    (a; Easy; p. 359)

39) Which type of promotion is designed to increase awareness and strengthen loyalty to a brand?
    a) consumer franchise-building
    b) consumer sales-building
    c) retailer generated
    d) nonfranchise-building
    (a; Moderate; p. 338)

40) Which type of promotion is designed to create immediate sales rather than brand equity or loyalty?
    a) consumer franchise-building promotions
    b) trade promotions
    c) consumer sales-building promotions
    d) nonfranchise building promotions
    (c; Moderate; p. 338)

41)   Nearly 80% of all coupons are distributed by _____ .
       a) manufacturers
       b) wholesalers
       c) retailers
       d) Internet companies
(a; Moderate; p. 339)

42)   A bounce-back coupon is _____ .
       a) not immediately redeemable
       b) not normally distributed by a manufacturer
       c) a form of premium
       d) used when the consumer purchases the product
(a; Moderate; p. 340)

43)   When time-share properties offer to let you stay for a night or weekend on the condition
       you listen to a sales pitch, they are using the consumer promotion technique of _____ .
       a) sampling
       b) a premium
       c) price-off
       d) coupon
(a; Moderate; pp. 336-338)

44)   A coupon for $1.00 off on golf balls placed on a golf towel is _____ .
       a) a response offer
       b) cross-ruffing
       c) a premium
       d) a bonus offer
(b; Moderate; p. 340)

45)   Making a copy of a coupon and then redeeming it for cash is an example of _____ .
       a) mass cutting
       b) counterfeiting
       c) misredemption
       d) standard industry practice
(b; Moderate; p. 342)

46)   A 50-cent coupon for a 16-ounce can that is redeemed for a 12-ounce can purchase is an
       example of _____ .
       a) coupon flexibility
       b) mass cutting
       c) retail discounting
       d) misredemption
(d; Moderate; p. 342)

47) Of the following groups, which has a lower record of redeeming coupons?
   a) p price-conscious consumers
   b) Caucasians
   c) females
   d) Hispanics
(d; Moderate; p. 341)

48) A coupon for a brand that a consumer already uses regularly will be _____ .
   a) more attractive to the consumer
   b) less attractive to the consumer
   c) unlikely to have an impact
   d) ignored due to issues of familiarity
(a; Moderate; p. 341)

49) Which requires the consumer to pay a small amount for a premium?
   a) in-package premium
   b) on-package premium
   c) store premium
   d) self-liquidating premium
(d; Moderate; p. 344)

50) A Cracker Jack prize is _____ .
   a) a bonus pack
   b) an in-package premium
   c) an on-package premium
   d) a self-liquidating premium
(b; Moderate; p. 343)

51) The two primary problems associated with premiums are _____ .
   a) short life spans and costs
   b) consumer indifference and clutter
   c) negative effects on brand image and recall
   d) perceptions of inequity in brand comparisons
(a; Moderate; p. 344)

52) Which does not match a sweepstakes?
   a) odds of winning must be published
   b) does not require a skill to be exhibited
   c) requires a purchase to enter
   d) the prize should have extrinsic value
(c; Moderate; p. 346)

53) Which does not match a contest?
   a) no purchase required to enter in any state
   b) probability of winning cannot easily be calculated
   c) creates intrinsic value for those who enter
   d) often requires a judge to decide the winner
(a; Moderate; p. 346)

54) Winning a trip to Nashville to record a song based on a singing contest is _____ .
   a) a prize with both extrinsic and intrinsic value
   b) a prize with no extrinsic value, only intrinsic
   c) a prize based on making a purchase in order to enter the contest
   d) a prize with a high extrinsic value, but little intrinsic value
(a; Moderate; p. 346)

55) Which is not an important characteristic of a rebate program?
   a) visibility
   b) brand equity
   c) perceived newness
   d) an impact
(b; Moderate; p. 349)

56) Free medicine to a doctor is an example of _____ .
   a) direct sampling
   b) response sampling
   c) professional sampling
   d) selective sampling
(c; Moderate; p. 351)

57) Placing a sample bar of soap in every mail box within a 10-block area is an example of _____ .
   a) direct sampling
   b) cross-ruff sampling
   c) selective sampling
   d) response sampling
(a; Moderate; p. 350)

58) If Colgate packages two tubes of toothpaste together to sell at a special price, it is an example of a _____ .
   a) cross-ruff pack
   b) rebate pack
   c) bonus pack
   d) price discount
(c; Moderate; p. 352)

59) Price-off offers are best for _____ .
   a) building firm image
   b) increasing store traffic and generating sales
   c) high involvement products
   d) consumers who are not price sensitive
(b; Moderate; p. 354)

60) Which country has the lowest coupon redemption rate?
   a) Italy
   b) Spain
   c) England
   d) United States
(c; Challenging; p. 358)

61) When Colgate promotes a new tooth-whitening product using discounts to retail stores and prizes to customers to create immediate sales, the approach is primarily _____ .
   a) franchise building
   b) sales building
   c) territory building
   d) brand-equity building
(b; Challenging; p. 338)

62) Which is a U-pon?
   a) FSI coupon
   b) Bounce-back coupon
   c) Internet-issued coupon
   d) Electronically-issued coupon
(d; Challenging; p. 341)

63) Coupon attractiveness is determined by all of the following except _____ .
   a) face value
   b) distribution method
   c) whether it is for a preferred brand or one in a consumer's evoked set
   d) match of the coupon's face value to the target market
(a; Challenging; p. 342)

64) Which is the best type of coupon to encourage brand switching?
   a) instant redemption coupon
   b) bounce-back coupon
   c) scanner -delivered coupon
   d) FSI
(c; Challenging; p. 340)

65) A pocket pager given as a gift for test driving a car is an example of a _____ .
   a) free-in-the-mail premium
   b) store or manufacturer premium
   c) self-liquidating premium
   d) in- or on-package premium
   (b; Challenging; pp. 343-344)

66) Which of the following statements is false?
   a) Premiums of higher quality lead to better response rates.
   b) Premiums add value to a product.
   c) Premiums reinforce the brand's image.
   d) Premiums build short-term profits.
   (d; Challenging; pp. 344-345)

67) The two primary goals of contests and sweepstakes are to _____ .
   a) build brand equity and boost sales
   b) boost sales and profits
   c) overcome advertising clutter and increase inquiries
   d) encourage customer traffic and boost sales
   (d; Challenging; p. 348)

68) Which of the following features is least likely to improve a contest's success?
   a) tie-ins with other companies
   b) increasing the values of prizes over time
   c) increasing the number of contests per year
   d) utilizing POPs and other advertising devices to promote the contest
   (c; Challenging; p. 348)

69) A small perfume sample in a magazine is _____ .
   a) a direct sampling program
   b) a response sampling program
   c) a media sampling program
   d) a selective sample program
   (c; Challenging; p. 351)

70) Which of the following statements is not true?
   a) Bonus packs appeal to price-sensitive consumers.
   b) Bonus packs rarely attract new customers.
   c) Bonus packs can lead to brand switching.
   d) Bonus packs can pre-empt the competition.
   (a; Challenging; pp. 353-354)

71) Which of the following statements is true?
   a) A price-off program is effective for individuals that have a high degree of brand loyalty to a competing brand.
   b) A price-off program has little impact on sales.
   c) A price-off program usually boosts sales, but it can hurt profits.
   d) A price-off program decreases price sensitivity over time.
(c; Challenging; pp. 353-354)

72) Which of the following statement is false?
   a) A price-off program can increase store traffic.
   b) A price-off program can generate sales.
   c) A price-off program has the least immediate reward compared to contests, sweepstakes and rebates.
   d) A price-off program should not target loyal users, but rather brand switchers.
(c; Challenging; pp. 353-354)

73) Which of the following is an intercompany tie-in promotion?
   a) Betty Crocker with Tyson
   b) a Whopper and onion rings at Burger King
   c) Pepsi and Diet Pepsi
   d) a double feature at the movies
(a; Challenging; p. 355)

74) Which of the following types of consumers responds best to coupons and premiums?
   a) Promotion-prone consumers
   b) brand-loyal consumers
   c) brand-image consumers
   d) price-sensitive consumers
(a; Challenging; p. 355)

75) John Deere offers to each tractor dealer that orders a new tractor a vintage toy tractor that can be displayed, sold, or given to a dealer's best customers. This promotion is an example of a business-to-business _____ .
   a) sampling
   b) bonus pack
   c) premium
   d) rebate
(c; Challenging; p. 357)

76) Folks Southern Kitchen advertises in the local newspaper a special $5.99 lunch special at any of its outlets during March. This promotion is an example of a _____ .
   a) coupon
   b) sampling
   c) premium
   d) price-off
(d; Challenging; p. 353-354)

77) Vanish has a $1.00-off coupon attached to the outside of the Vanish container that can be easily removed. This is an example of a(n) _____ .
   a) instant redemption coupon
   b) bounce-back coupon
   c) cross-ruffing coupon
   d) response-offer coupon
(a; Challenging; p. 340)

78) Fisher Boy has both a 55 cents-off coupon and an entry form for a sweepstakes in an advertisement. This is an example of a(n) _____ .
   a) intercompany tie-in
   b) intracompany tie-in
   c) overlay
   d) bonus pack
(c; Challenging; p. 354-355)

79) Among the countries listed below, overall redemption rates for consumer promotions are the lowest in _____ .
   a) England
   b) Italy
   c) Spain
   d) United States
(d; Challenging; p. 358)

80) Approximately 80% of all coupons are redeemed by _____ .
   a) Brand-loyal customers
   b) Promotion-prone customers
   c) Price-sensitive customers
   d) retail stores
(a; Challenging; p. 341)

Short-Answer Questions

81) What are the major forms of coupons?

Instant redemption, bounce-back, scanner-delivered, cross-ruffing, response offer, and electronically delivered U-pons.
(Easy; pp. 340-341)

82) What problems are associated with coupons?

Reduced revenues, mass cutting, counterfeiting, and misredemptions.
(Easy; pp. 341-342)

83) What is the primary difference between a contest and a sweepstakes?

A contest requires a skill or entry of some sort. Many require purchases to enter. Sweepstakes are games of chance where consumers may enter as many times as they wish.
(Easy; p. 346)

84) How can coupons be made more attractive to consumers?

Higher face value, FSI distribution, and a preferred brand coupon is more attractive.
(Moderate; p. 342)

85) What are the four major types of premiums?

1. free-in-the-mail
2. in- or on-package
3. store or manufacturer
4. self-liquidating
(Moderate; pp. 343-344)

86) For contests and sweepstakes, what is the difference between extrinsic value and intrinsic value in prizes?

Extrinsic value is the actual attractiveness of the item. Intrinsic values are associated with playing or participating.
(Moderate; p. 346)

87) What are the characteristics of effective refund and rebate programs?

Visibility, perceived newness, impact.
(Moderate; p. 349)

88) Name the various forms of sampling.

- In-store distribution
- Direct sampling
- Response samples
- Cross-ruff samples
- Media sampling
- Professional samples
- Selective samples
(Challenging; p. 350)

89)   What are the major objectives of bonus packs?

- Increase product usage
- Match or pre-empt competition
- Consumer stockpiling of the product
- Develop customer loyalty
- Encourage brand switching

(Challenging; p. 352)

90)   How can a company build a successful premium program?

- Match the premium to the target market
- Reinforce the firm's image with the premium
- Tie the premium to the firm's products
- Make the premium in sufficient quality
- Integrate with the overall IMC approach

(Challenging; pp. 344-345)

CHAPTER 12
PERSONAL SELLING, DATABASE MARKETING, AND CUSTOMER RELATIONSHIP MANAGEMENT

True-False Questions

1)   Personal selling is sometimes called the "last three feet" of the marketing function because of the relationship between selling and advertising.
(False; Easy; p. 368)

2)   In a single transaction, high-pressure tactics are the most effective, especially in the long term.
(False; Easy; p. 370)

3)   Cross-selling is marketing an unrelated item following the purchase of a good or service.
(True; easy; p. 371)

4)   Occasional transactions in business-to-business settings are similar to modified rebuy situations.
(True; Easy; p. 372)

5)   Geocoding is adding geographic codes to customer records.
(True; Easy; p. 382)

6)   Data mining normally involves building profiles of consumer groups and preparing models that predict future purchase behaviors.
(True; Easy; p. 383)

7)   One of the keys to customer relationship management (CRM) programs is to differentiate customers in terms of their needs and their value to the company.
(True; Easy; p.390)

8)   In-bound telemarketing is receiving calls and inquiries from outside customers.
(True; Moderate; p. 369)

9)   In the problem recognition stage of a retail sale, the representative should strongly urge the customer to focus on one product that will best resolve the problem.
(False; Moderate; p. 370)

10)   Qualifying prospects in business-to-business sales is the process of compiling a complete list of potential customers.
(False; Moderate; p. 374)

11) Many salespeople skip the knowledge acquisition stage of selling and move directly to the sales call because this is where commissions are gained.
(True; Moderate; p. 375)

12) In a stimulus-response approach to selling, the idea is to fully understand the customer's needs and customize solutions.
(False; Moderate; p. 376)

13) Digital direct-to-press is only used in business-to-business marketing due to its costs.
(False; Moderate; p. 387)

14) Record and book clubs that send out monthly mailings of books and records to purchase are using a permissions marketing program.
(True; Challenging; pp. 388-389)

15) Customer relationship management (CRM) works best when a company can modify aspects of its goods or services to fit customers, especially when those customers have very little differentiation in their needs.
(False; Challenging; p. 390)

16) Out-bound telemarketing calls are invasive, annoying, and yet successful for many firms.
(True; Challenging; p. 369)

17) Repeat transactions and contractual agreements often build high levels of trust between the buyer and seller.
(False; Challenging; p. 373)

18) During the knowledge acquisition stage of the b-to-b selling prospect, the salesperson needs to determine the prospect's perception of risk in switching vendors.
(True; Challenging; pp. 375-376)

19) Cultural assimilators are usually not necessary in personal selling because international business has become more standardized in the past decade.
(False; Challenging; p. 379)

20) In terms of direct marketing, ride-alongs are materials that are placed with a company's own catalog or direct-mail pieces, such as a record club's catalog.
(False; Challenging; p. 387)

21) Moderate users of a good or service are most likely to be enticed by a frequency program.
(True; Challenging; p. 389)

Multiple-Choice Questions

22) An order-taker salesperson is most likely to also be a _____ .
    a) telemarketer
    b) business-to-business rep
    c) cashier
    d) prospector
(c; Easy; p. 369)

23) Which of the following types of salespeople would take inquiry phone calls?
    a) missionary salesperson
    b) in-bound telemarketer
    c) out-bound telemarketer
    d) prospector
(b; Easy; p. 369)

24) Inbound telemarketing calls are a good time to _____ .
    a) point out the disadvantages of a competitor's product
    b) discover consumer needs
    c) display the product's advantages
    d) cross-sell additional goods or services
(d; Easy; p. 371)

25) In terms of b-to-b buying situations, occasional transactions are normally _____ .
    a) new buy situations
    b) modified rebuy situations
    c) straight rebuy situations
    d) any of the three situations
(b; Easy; p. 372)

26) An EDI relationship is _____ .
    a) the sharing of data
    b) the sharing of sales reps
    c) the sharing of telemarketing information
    d) the same as a contractual relationship
(a; Easy; p. 373)

27) When prospecting, which is the least effective?
    a) current customers
    b) trade shows
    c) advertising
    d) cold canvassing
(d; Easy; p. 374)

28) A need-satisfaction sales approach focuses on the customer's _____ .
   a) response to a canned sales approach
   b) strategic value orientation
   c) reaction to competition
   d) desire for solutions to specific needs
   (d; Easy; p. 376)

29) A mission-sharing sales approach is most similar to _____ .
   a) price-quality relationships
   b) joint-venture projects
   c) missionary sales
   d) modified rebuy situations
   (b; Easy; p. 376)

30) The selling approach that requires the selling organization to analyze the buyer's operation before making the sales presentation is _____ .
   a) stimulus-response
   b) need-satisfaction
   c) problem-solution
   d) mission-sharing
   (c; Easy; p. 376)

31) Which of the following is not internal data?
   a) scanner data
   b) telephone numbers collected from sales contacts
   c) addresses recorded from checks
   d) commercial database service information
   (d; Easy; p. 381)

32) The process of building profiles of customers from a firm's database is called _____ .
   a) data warehousing
   b) direct marketing
   c) a commercial database service
   d) data mining
   (d; Easy; p. 383)

33) Mail, catalogs, telemarketing, and mass media can all be used for _____ .
   a) direct marketing
   b) permission marketing
   c) data mining
   d) relationship marketing
   (a; Easy; p. 385)

34) A card pack is _____ .
   a) telemarketing to a stack of cards containing prospects
   b) direct-marketing materials placed in mail-order fulfillment packages
   c) direct marketing materials containing business reply cards in a plastic pack
   d) a form of ride-along program
(c; Easy; p. 387)

35) Response rates are often higher for permissions marketing programs because _____.
   a) consumers are receiving marketing material they have given permission for
   b) consumers are high-frequency purchasers
   c) consumers can reject any offer that is made
   d) consumers are contacted only by mail
(a; Easy; p. 388)

36) The program designed to build long-term loyalty and bonds with customers, using a personal selling touch combined by effective technology is known as _____ .
   a) permission marketing
   b) direct marketing
   c) customer relationship management
   d) frequency marketing
(c; Easy; p. 390)

37) The average number of visits made by a customer times the average amount of money spent per visit calculates _____ .
   a) consumer's expectancy value
   b) a customer's lifetime value
   c) a customer's visitation value
   d) return traffic count
(b; Easy; p. 390)

38) In terms of the consumer buying process, the best time to specifically sell a product's advantages is during _____ .
   a) problem recognition
   b) information search
   c) evaluation of alternatives
   d) post-purchase evaluations
(c; Moderate; p. 370)

39) In the business-to-business buying situation, a single transaction approach may be used effectively in a _____ .
   a) straight rebuy situation
   b) modified rebuy situation
   c) new buy situation
   d) any of the buying situations
(d; Moderate; p. 372)

40) Typical objectives for an IMC database program do not include _____ .
   a) providing useful information about the firm's customers
   b) revealing contact points that can be used in direct marketing programs
   c) creating information about why customers purchase the products they do
   d) making informal contact with customers
(d; Moderate; p. 381)

41) From the following terms, which term does not fit with the others?
   a) missionary salesperson
   b) order-getter
   c) merchandiser
   d) detailer
(b; Moderate; p. 371)

42) Extrinsic value buyers _____ .
   a) focus on price
   b) focus mostly on product attributes
   c) seek information about new vendors
   d) seek partnerships with suppliers
(b; Moderate; p. 376)

43) Which usually involves the most face-to-face contact with customers?
   a) field sales
   b) in-house sales
   c) Internet sales
   d) telemarketing
(a; Moderate; p. 372)

44) Which is the most likely to use Internet and e-mail programs to communicate?
   a) trust relationships
   b) modified rebuys
   c) EDI relationships
   d) contractual agreements
(c; Moderate; p. 373)

45) From the following types of buyers, which would be most interested in price?
   a) intrinsic value buyers
   b) extrinsic value buyers
   c) strategic value buyers
   d) EDI relationship partners
(a; Moderate; p. 376)

46) Which would be most likely to use a stimulus-response sales approach?
   a) missionary salesperson
   b) order-taker
   c) telemarketer
   d) engineers and teams
   (c; Moderate; p. 376)

47) Which sales approach is most likely to be used in a strategic partnership?
   a) stimulus-response
   b) need-satisfaction
   c) problem-solution
   d) mission-sharing
   (d; Moderate; p. 376)

48) Which is often the case in a follow-up to a business-to-business sale?
   a) The rep has lost interest because the commission has been earned.
   b) The company will want to re-negotiate the sales contract.
   c) The buyer will seek out additional information about competitors.
   d) The vendor will redefine its IMC approach.
   (a; Moderate; p. 377)

49) As technology continues to evolve, many experts expect _____ .
   a) more sales positions
   b) fewer sales positions
   c) about the same sales positions
   d) fewer retail opportunities
   (b; Moderate; p. 378)

50) Direct-marketing programs create _____ .
   a) one-to-one contacts with customers
   b) frequency programs
   c) re-analysis of databases
   d) new mass media messages
   (a; Moderate; p. 385)

51) With geocoding, a company can add to each customer's records _____ .
   a) demographic information and lifestyle data
   b) total purchases made at each retail outlet in the area
   c) demographic and political information
   d) a composite analysis of his or her neighbors
   (a; Moderate; p. 382)

52) Which is data mining?
   a) collecting addresses and zip codes
   b) reviewing past purchases of a product
   c) building customer groups and models that predict their purchases
   d) selecting cities for data analysis
(c; Moderate; p. 383)

53) Which is not true concerning permission marketing?
   a) The company does not intrude with unwanted junk mail.
   b) Response rates are higher because consumers have given permission.
   c) Marketing costs are increased due to greater records that must be kept.
   d) Consumers enjoy not being bombarded with catalogs and telemarketing calls.
(c; Moderate; p. 388)

54) Which is not a reason that frequency programs become more expensive?
   a) companies overestimate the cost
   b) members do not accumulate enough free merchandise or rewards
   c) record-keeping and mailing costs
   d) free tickets
(a; Moderate; p. 389)

55) When differentiating customers in terms of needs and value as part of a (customer relationship management (CRM) program, which two metrics are calculated?
   a) earnings per share and markup per customer
   b) markup per sale and cost of the sale
   c) customer lifetime value and share of customer
   d) cost of permissions minus revenue per customer
(c; Moderate; p. 390)

56) Which is not a key technological underpinning to a customer relationship management (CRM) program?
   a) database technology
   b) interactivity through Web site
   c) mass customization technology
   d) access to fax and teleconference
(d; Moderate; p. 391)

57) Which type of salesperson works at discount stores like Wal-Mart?
   a) missionary
   b) order taker
   c) strategic
   d) telemarketer
(b; Challenging; p. 369)

58) A salesperson showing a prospective buyer the superiority of the Ford Taurus as compared to the Toyota Camry would take place during _____ .
   a) problem recognition
   b) information search
   c) evaluation of alternatives
   d) purchase decision
(c; Challenging; p. 370)

59) Selling an insurance policy following the opening of a checking account at a bank would be an example of _____ .
   a) missionary sales
   b) trust relationships
   c) cross-selling
   d) strategic partnerships with individual customers
(c; Challenging; p. 371)

60) The manufacturer's dilemma in personal selling is that _____ .
   a) most salespeople are incompetent
   b) most customers base sales decisions on advertising by retailers
   c) most customers make final purchase decisions in the store
   d) most customers are strongly influenced by order-takers
(c; Challenging; p. 371)

61) Which type of sales would involve responding to or taking an order from an established customer?
   a) new buy
   b) field sales
   c) missionary sales
   d) in-house sales
(d; Challenging; p. 372)

62) When a wireless phone company combines with an Internet access company to develop a plan to reach certain business customers, the relationship is _____ .
   a) an EDI relationship
   b) a trust relationship
   c) a joint partnership
   d) a strategic partnership
(d; Challenging; p. 373)

63) In the selling process, the knowledge acquisition stage does not involve _____ .
   a) knowing the prospect's customers
   b) prospecting for new potential customers
   c) assessing customer needs
   d) identifying customer benefits and product attributes crucial to the buyer
(b; Challenging; p. 375)

64) In a new buy situation, the best approach is probably going to be _____ .
   a) stimulus-response
   b) need-satisfaction
   c) problem-solving
   d) mission-sharing
   (c; Challenging; p. 376)

65) EDI technology makes it possible for computers to _____ .
   a) place and take orders
   b) contact customers by phone
   c) increase the size of the sales force
   d) dissolve unprofitable partnerships
   (a; Challenging; p. 373)

66) CACI Coder/plus is a form of _____ .
   a) internally generated data
   b) governmental data
   c) survey data
   d) geocoding data
   (d; Challenging; pp. 382-383)

67) When is an inducement such as a gift, information, or cash offered in a permission marketing program?
   a) when obtaining the initial permission of the consumer
   b) while building a database
   c) while offering the consumer a full curriculum of information
   d) at the conclusion of the program
   (a; Challenging; p. 388)

68) The Book of the Month Club is an example of _____ .
   a) digital direct-to-press
   b) relationship marketing
   c) direct marketing
   d) permission marketing
   (d; Challenging; p. 388)

69) The highest level of involvement and loyalty occurs at which stage in a permission marketing program?
   a) when obtaining the initial permission
   b) when reinforcing the incentives
   c) when increasing the permission level
   d) when leveraging the information
   (d; Challenging; pp. 388-389)

70) Which is false concerning customer relationship management programs?
 a) they succeed nearly every time they are implemented
 b) it is crucial to change the organization to match the program in order to succeed
 c) the company must be customer, not technology driven in order to succeed
 d) the program will not succeed if customers feel they are being pressured
(a; Challenging; p. 391)

71) A hair stylist in a beauty salon that tries to cross-sell hair products while he or she is cutting a customer's hair is serving the role of a(n) _____ .
 a) order getter
 b) order taker
 c) field salesperson
 d) missionary salesperson
(a; Challenging; p. 372)

72) In addition to a sales call, potential customers of Polycom's Videoconferencing System can contact Polycom through the Internet or by calling a toll-free number. This is an example of the b-to-b selling trend of _____ .
 a) decline in the number of salespeople
 b) expansion of sales channels
 c) increase in long-term relationships and strategic partnerships
 d) increase in team selling
(b; Challenging; p. 378)

73) All of the b-to-b personal selling trends listed below are expected to increase except
_____ .
 a) the number of salespeople
 b) the number of sales channels
 c) the use of long-term relationships and strategic partnerships
 d) the use of the team selling approach
(a; Challenging; p. 378)

74) In developing a database, all of the information below would be internal data a company should have except _____ .
 a) where customers live
 b) what customers have purchased and how much
 c) how often they have purchased
 d) what type of media they tend to watch
(d; Challenging; p. 381)

75) Data mining can be used for all of the following purposes <u>except</u> _____ .
   a) develop profiles of a firm's best customers
   b) develop profiles of customers who tend to purchase competing brands
   c) identify current customers who fit the profile of a firm's best customers
   d) identify current customers who would be good prospects for cross-selling other products

(b; Challenging; p. 383)

76) The most common form of direct marketing is _____ .
   a) direct mail
   b) catalogs
   c) telemarketing
   d) mass-media

(a; Challenging; p. 386)

77) Many firms have launched into Customer Relationship Management programs because of the potential to develop strong ties with customers ; unfortunately, according to the Gartner Group, the percentage that fail is approximately _____ .
   a) 25%
   b) 40%
   c) 55%
   d) 70%

(c; Challenging; p. 391)

78) In developing a CRM program, the share of customer term means _____ .
   a) the potential value that could be added to a given customer's lifetime value
   b) the lifelong earning of a customer
   c) the share of a customer's income that is spent on a particular product
   d) the percentage of time spent on acquiring the customer's loyalty

(a; Challenging; p. 390)

79) When a customer at a retail store says, "I'm not sure I really need a new TV right now," she is in which stage of the consumer buying process?
   a) problem recognition
   b) information search
   c) evaluation of alternatives
   d) purchase decision

(a; Challenging; p. 370)

80) A customer at a retail store just purchased a Peerless faucet. Cross-selling has occurred when the salesperson _____ .
   a) asks the customer to fill out a customer information card for a free drawing
   b) shows the customer how to install the faucet
   c) sells the customer a water purifier to go with the new faucet
   d) contacts Peerless to make sure the faucet will work in the customer's home

(c; Challenging; p. 371)

81)   What are the four main kinds of retail selling?

    1. Selling in shops and stores
    2. Selling services and merchandise to accompany services
    3. Telemarketing
    4. Other retail sales activities, such as stocking shelves or offering advice
(Easy; p. 369)

82)   What are the stages of the purchasing process?

    1. Problem recognition
    2. Information search
    3. Evaluation of alternatives
    4. Purchase decision
    5. Post-purchase evaluation
(Easy; p. 370)

83)   What are the three primary forms of business-to-business selling?

    1. Field sales
    2. In-house sales
    3. Telemarketing and Internet programs
(Easy; p. 372)

84)   What kinds of buyer seller relationship are present in business-to-business selling? Rank them from lowest to highest.

    1. Single transaction
    2. Occasional transaction
    3. Repeat transaction
    4. Contractual agreements
    5. Trust relationships
    6. Electronic Data Interchange (EDI) relationships
    7. Strategic partnerships
(Moderate; p. 372)

85) What are the steps of the personal selling process in business-to-business relationships?

1. Identifying prospects
2. Qualifying prospects
3. Knowledge acquisition
4. Developing a sales approach
5. Sales presentation
6. Follow-up

(Moderate; p. 376)

86) What are the steps involved in developing a strategic partnership?

1. Awareness – where the customer learns of the vendor's capabilities.
2. Exploration – or the initial trial period at the transaction level with no or limited commitment by both parties.
3. Expansion – where interactions, commitments, and profits of both parties increase. A contractual arrangement may also be reached.
4. Commitment – in which the agreement between the parties is exclusive and trusting and may involve EDI interchanges.
5. Partnership – with sharing of people, resources, data, and combined missions, designed to accomplish unified goals that benefit both parties.

(Challenging; p. 373)

87) What methods are available for identifying business-to-business sales prospects?

- Current customers
- Databases
- Trade shows
- Advertising and Internet inquiries
- Consumer sales promotion responses
- Vendors
- Channel members
- Networking
- Cold canvassing

(Challenging; p. 374)

88)	What are the new trends in business-to-business personal selling?

- Increased use of technology
- Decline in the number of salespeople
- Expanding channels
- More long-term partnerships
- Team selling approaches used more frequently
- More database customer segmentation
- International concerns

(Challenging; p. 378)

89)	Name the steps involved in developing an IMC database.

1. Determine objectives
2. Collect data
3. Build a data warehouse
4. Mine data for information
5. Develop a marketing program
6. Evaluate the marketing program and data warehouse

(Challenging; p. 380)

90)	What four steps are involved in creating a customer relationship management (CRM) program?

1. Identify the company's customers
2. Differentiate customers in terms of their needs and their value to the selling company
3. Interact with customers in ways that improve cost efficiency and the effectiveness of the interactions
4. Customize some aspects of the products or services being offered to the customer

(Challenging, pp. 390-391)

CHAPTER 13
PUBLIC RELATIONS, REGULATIONS, AND SPONSORSHIP PROGRAMS

True-False Questions

1) The public relations department is the unit in the firm that manages items such as advertising and consumer promotions.
    (False; Easy; p. 403)

2) The first step a firm can take to end an FTC investigation of a complaint is the signing of a consent order, if a violation has occurred.
    (True; Easy; p. 418)

3) A stakeholder is a person or group with a vested interest in an organization's well-being.
    (True; Easy; p. 404)

4) Cause-related marketing is an internal program working with company employees.
    (False; Easy; p. 408)

5) In terms of public relations' tools, internal media include bulletin boards, e-mail list serves, memos, and letters.
    (True; Easy; p. 414)

6) The difference between event marketing and sponsorship marketing is the duration of the program being featured.
    (False; Easy; p. 424)

7) Labor unions and shareholders are internal stakeholders or publics.
    (True; Moderate; p. 404)

8) Cross-promotions are tie-ins with event marketing programs.
    (True; Moderate; p. 425)

9) When a substantial number of people are misled by a series of commercials, it is a violation of the Wheeler-Lea Amendment.
    (True; Moderate; p. 416)

10) For consumers who find an advertisement to be offensive, the FTC would be a legitimate place to file a complaint.
    (False; Moderate; p. 418)

11) The FTC can order civil penalties for violating consent orders.
    (False; Moderate; p. 418)

12) The FTC has the power to order firms to prepare and disseminate corrective advertising.
(True; Moderate; p. 419)

13) The National Advertising Review Board (NARB) seldom refers cases to the FTC.
(True; Moderate; p. 422)

14) A complaint filed with the National Advertising Division (NAD) of the Better Business Bureau regarding an unsubstantiated advertising claim would be dismissed because substantiation is not a criterion.
(False; Moderate; p. 421)

15) It is easier for the public relations department to access internal stakeholders as opposed to external stakeholders.
(True; Challenging; p. 405)

16) The majority of consumers are willing to switch retailers if the firm has an association with a good cause.
(True; Challenging; p. 408)

17) A person targeted by a mail fraud campaign should contact the Federal Communication Commission (FCC).
(False; Challenging; p. 417)

18) Tiger Woods' entry into the Buick Open as a representative of the company is an example of event marketing.
(False; Challenging; p. 422)

19) A rodeo sponsored by Lee Jeans is an example of event marketing.
(True; Challenging; p. 424)

20) Advertising dog food at a dog show is an example of a cross promotion.
(False; Challenging; p. 425)

Multiple-Choice Questions

21) Which would be most likely to oversee both the public relations department and the marketing department?
   a) department of communications
   b) department of advertising
   c) department of specialty events
   d) department of production
(a; Easy; p. 403)

22) In terms of goals for public relations, a hit is _____ .
   a) an advertisement that is successful
   b) a consumer promotions' tie in with publicity
   c) mention of the company's name in a news story
   d) an advertising slogan with high recall
(c; Easy; p. 403)

23) Which is not considered an internal stakeholder?
   a) employees
   b) labor unions
   c) shareholders
   d) customers
(d; Easy; p. 404)

24) Which is not considered an external stakeholder?
   a) labor unions
   b) channel members
   c) customers
   d) the media
(a; Easy; p. 404)

25) Accepting blame for an event, offering an apology, or forcefully refuting the charges is an example of _____ .
   a) impression management
   b) crisis management
   c) an entitling
   d) an enhancement
(b; Easy; p. 411)

26) Which public relations tool is mostly internally oriented?
   a) press release
   b) company newsletter
   c) financial statement
   d) contact point
(b; Easy; p. 414)

27) The Wheeler-Lea Amendment to the FTC Act prohibits _____ .
   a) excessive advertising to children
   b) false and misleading advertising
   c) puffery and comparative advertising
   d) stereotyping in advertising
(b; Easy; p. 416)

28) The Federal Trade Commission regulates _____ .
   a) the packaging and labeling of products
   b) the use of mailing materials in advertising
   c) the television, radio, and telephone industries
   d) food quality and labeling
(c; Easy; p. 418)

29) Puffery is _____ .
   a) a deliberate attempt to mislead and deceive
   b) any illegal marketing activity
   c) increased product prices to cover advertising costs
   d) an exaggerated claim with no overt attempt to mislead or deceive
(d; Easy; p. 416)

30) The agency with the greatest degree of jurisdiction over marketing and advertising is the
   _____ .
   a) FTC
   b) FCC
   c) United States Postal Service
   d) FDA
(a; Easy; p. 417)

31) The agency that monitors advertising on food packages and advertisements for drugs is
   the _____ .
   a) FTC
   b) FCC
   c) United States Postal Service
   d) FDA
(d; Easy; p. 417)

32) An administrative complaint is _____ .
   a) a formal proceeding before an administrative law judge used by the FTC
   b) a form of cease and desist order
   c) rarely used by the FTC
   d) used by the NARB when the NAD cannot solve a complaint
(a; Easy; p. 418)

33) A trade regulatory ruling by the FTC applies to _____ .
   a) wholesalers
   b) international companies
   c) an industry
   d) retailers
(c; Easy; p. 419)

34) When a company pays money to sponsor someone or some group, which is participating in an activity, it is called _____ .
   a) public relations
   b) advertising expenditures
   c) marketing myopia
   d) sponsorship marketing
(d; Easy; p. 422)

35) Sponsoring a team, group, or person or a specific venue is _____ .
   a) public relations
   b) sponsorship marketing
   c) event marketing
   d) marketing management
(b; Easy; p. 424)

36) When a company advertises, develops consumer promotions, such as a contest, and develops other marketing communications as a tie-in with an event marketing program, it is called _____ .
   a) a local promotion
   b) a corporate promotion
   c) an advertising promotion
   d) a cross-promotion
(d; Easy; p. 425)

37) "Turf wars" can develop between _____ .
   a) the public relations department and the marketing department
   b) internal and external publics
   c) the department of communications and the marketing department
   d) market analysts and the marketing department
(a; Moderate; p. 403)

38) In terms of measuring the impact of public relations, a "hit" can enhance _____ .
   a) the use of a tagline
   b) brand awareness
   c) company policies
   d) stock dividends
(b; Moderate; p. 403)

39) Profit statements, publicity, and proxy votes directly impact which kind of stakeholder?
   a) internal
   b) external
   c) corporate
   d) media
(a; Moderate; p. 405)

40) Special interest groups are _____ .
    a) internal stakeholders
    b) disgruntled employees
    c) external stakeholders
    d) governmental stakeholders
(c; Moderate; p. 407)

41) When Tang noted in company commercials that the product was the official drink of NASA during the first moon landing, the approach being used is called _____ .
    a) crisis management
    b) impression management
    c) an enhancement
    d) an Internet intervention
(c; Moderate; pp. 412-413)

42) Believing that Wheaties may help make you a champion, since so many successful athletes have endorsed the cereal, is the result of which process?
    a) impression management
    b) acclimation
    c) entitlings
    d) reinforcement
(c; Moderate; pp. 412-413)

43) If negative publicity is combated in an Internet chat room, the approach being used is called _____.
    a) impression management
    b) entitling
    c) enhancement
    d) an Internet intervention
(d; Moderate; p. 413)

44) Soft information, such as articles about company picnics, would be found in _____ .
    a) newsletters
    b) press releases
    c) communications audits
    d) contact points
(a; Moderate; p. 414)

45) Which is true about media news releases?
    a) they should be sent out as often as possible
    b) they should be written by advertising creatives
    c) sending out too many will cause them to be ignored
    d) most news organizations receive very few of them, so they invite submissions regularly
(c; Moderate; p. 415)

46) Companies not satisfied with the ruling of the full FTC commission can appeal to the U.S. Court of Appeals. The danger for companies in appealing to the Court of Appeals is that _____ .
   a) the company does not have the opportunity to present oral arguments
   b) the cease and desist orders are normally upheld
   c) a company may be ordered to pay civil penalties
   d) the decision is not binding
   (c; Moderate; p. 418)

47) The FTC test of substantiation is _____ .
   a) a comparison of marketing claims made by competing firms
   b) the use of a code of ethics
   c) using reliable and competent evidence as the basis of a marketing claim
   d) normally not a component in an FTC case regarding deceptive advertising
   (c; Moderate; p. 420)

48) Paying for entry fees into a league and uniforms for a little league soccer program is an example of _____ .
   a) sponsorship marketing
   b) event marketing
   c) cause-related marketing
   d) an ineffective contact point
   (a; Moderate; p. 422)

49) Paying for an advertisement promoting a concert tour by a band and creating tie-ins with company products at the concerts is an example of _____ .
   a) sponsorship marketing
   b) event marketing
   c) cause-related marketing
   d) musical marketing
   (a; Moderate; p. 423)

50) Conducting a health fair at a local hospital is an example of _____ .
   a) sponsorship marketing
   b) event marketing
   c) cause-related marketing
   d) tie-in marketing
   (b; Moderate; p. 424)

51) When McDonald's claims they have the best-tasting hamburgers, they are engaged in _____ .
   a) A code of ethics violation
   b) misleading and deceptive advertising
   c) puffery
   d) cross-promotions
   (c; Moderate; p. 416)

52) Word such as "best," "greatest," and "finest" are examples of _____ .
    a) deceptive advertising
    b) misleading advertising
    c) standard industry practices
    d) puffery
   (d; Moderate; p. 416)

53) If a customer is concerned about the labeling on a bag of potato chips, the regulatory agency that should be contacted is the _____ .
    a) FCC
    b) FDA
    c) FTC
    d) BATF
   (b; Moderate; p. 417)

54) Public complaints about the amount of violence on television would be sent to the _____ .
    a) FCC
    b) FDA
    c) FTC
    d) BATF
    (a; Moderate; p. 417)

55) When the FTC insists that a company stops making a false claim in an advertisement and that company agrees to stop, this is an example of _____ .
    a) a legal review
    b) a cease-and-desist order
    c) a case for the U.S. Postal Service
    d) a consent order
   (d; Moderate; p. 418)

56) If a consumer wants to know if people have complained about a particular health club being unsafe or unclean, he or she should contact the _____ .
    a) NAD
    b) FTC
    c) Better Business Bureau
    d) NARB
   (c; Moderate; p. 421)

57) A company stops using Styrofoam containers because they hurt the environment and starts using recycled paper is an example of _____ .
    a) event marketing
    b) green marketing
    c) altruistic effort
    d) cause-related marketing
   (b; Moderate; p. 409)

58)   A news story about the Ford Explorer's tire problems is an example of a(n) _____ .
         a) public relations' hit
         b) event
         c) negative tie-in
         d) negative cross-promotion
      (a; Challenging; p. 403)

59)   Which is not a stakeholder?
         a) suppliers of raw materials
         b) foreign governments for a non-international company
         c) the media
         d) contributors to a charity
      (b; Challenging; pp. 404-407)

60)   Drug and alcohol counseling for employees is an example of _____ .
         a) an external contact point
         b) an altruistic activity
         c) cause-related marketing
         d) adapting the IMC plan
      (b; Challenging p. 408)

61)   Showing only beautiful, happy people drinking beer in commercials is an example of
      _____ .
         a) impression management
         b) crisis management
         c) entitling
         d) enhancement
      (a; Challenging; p. 411)

62)   A local race car driver who displays advertising on the car is involved in _____ .
         a) sponsorship marketing
         b) event marketing
         c) mobile marketing
         d) cause-related marketing
      (a; Challenging; pp. 422-424)

63)   A Hispanic fiesta funded by a food company is an example of _____ .
         a) sponsorship marketing
         b) event marketing
         c) cause-related marketing
         d) a cross-promotion
      (b; Challenging; p. 424)

64) The Coca-Cola booth at spring break on South Padre Island is an example of _____ .
    a) sponsorship marketing
    b) event marketing
    c) specialty marketing
    d) a cross-promotion
(b; Challenging; p. 424)

65) Giving out samples of Pizza Hut products in conjunction with the debut of a motion picture that was funded by Pizza Hut is an example of _____ .
    a) sponsorship marketing
    b) event marketing
    c) specialty marketing
    d) a cross-promotion
(d; Challenging; p. 425)

66) In terms of a judgment by the FTC, which of the following would come first?
    a) administrative complaint
    b) cease-- and-desist order
    c) consent order
    d) court-ordered reparations
(c; Challenging; p. 418)

67) Which agency has the authority to order corrective advertising?
    a) FCC
    b) FTC
    c) FDA
    d) BAFT
(b; Challenging; p. 419)

68) The funeral industry was sanctioned by the FTC in 1984 and 1994 using a _____ .
    a) cease and-desist order
    b) consent order
    c) corrective advertising order
    d) trade regulation ruling
(d; Challenging; p. 419-420)

69) The substantiation test for false and misleading advertising requires _____ .
    a) scientific tests
    b) consumer testimonials
    c) competent and reliable evidence
    d) the average person to be convinced it is not false and misleading
(c; Challenging; p. 420)

70) The National Advertising Division (NAD) of the BBB becomes involved in all of the following except _____ .
   a) cases of mail fraud
   b) collecting information about misleading advertising
   c) negotiating modification of ads deemed to be misleading
   d) dismissing unsubstantiated complaints
(a; Challenging; p. 421)

71) An appeal of a decision by the National Advertising Division (NAD) would go to the _____ .
   a) United States Court of Appeals
   b) FTC
   c) NARB
   d) FCC
(c; Challenging; p. 421)

72) Biodegradable laundry detergent is an example of _____ .
   a) cause-related marketing
   b) event marketing
   c) green marketing
   d) positive public relations
(c; Challenging; p. 409)

73) Public relations' functions include all of the following except _____ .
   a) monitor internal and external publics
   b) provide positive information to each public that reinforces the IMC plan
   c) react quickly to any shift by any of the publics from the desired position
   d) provide the various publics with copies of any new IMC material before it is made public
(d; Challenging; p. 403)

74) Philip Morris sends out countertop placards to retailers suggesting that they ID any customer who looks younger than 27. This is an example of _____ .
   a) altruistic activities
   b) green marketing
   c) cause-related marketing
   d) impressions management
(d; Challenging; p. 411)

75) In terms of cause-related marketing, the highest percentage of Americans prefers that companies support causes that _____ .
   a) improve public schools
   b) support dropout prevention
   c) provide scholarships
   d) cleanup the environment
(a; Challenging; p. 408)

76) In terms of using an impressions management technique to respond to negative publicity, a company that makes the negative incident appear minor or trivial is using the remedial approach of _____ .
   a) expressions of innocence
   b) excuses
   c) justification
   d) apology
(c; Challenging; p. 412)

77) An advertisement or communication is deemed to be deceptive or misleading when _____ .
   a) the misrepresentation induces anyone to make a purchase
   b) a substantial number of people make a purchase
   c) a substantial number of people or the "typical person" is left with a false impression or misrepresentation that relates to the product
   d) a competing firm makes the same claim
(c; Challenging; p. 416)

78) Occasionally, the FTC bypasses the normal steps and will use the court system to stop unfair and deceptive advertising and communication practices when _____ .
   a) a company violates a FTC cease-and-desist order
   b) a full commission of the FTC is not available to hear a case
   c) a company violates a consent order
   d) a company appeals a consent order
(a; Challenging; pp. 418-419)

79) In terms of substantiation, if an advertiser uses expert endorsements, then statements in the advertisement must be based on _____ .
   a) legitimate tests performed by experts in the field
   b) the opinion of "typical persons" who would use the product
   c) truthful statements that represent the experts personal experience
   d) lab or engineering tests
(a; Challenging; p. 420)

80) In the last 25 years, the number of cases that the NARB has referred to the Federal Trade Commission is _____ .
   a) only 4
   b) about 25
   c) none because all cases are referred to the NAD
   d) large because rulings of the NARB are not binding, therefore most companies appeal the decision made
(a; Challenging; p. 4242

Short-Answer Questions

81) Who are the major internal stakeholders for a public relations department to consider?

- Employees
- Labor unions
- Shareholders

(Easy; pp. 404-405)

82) Describe sponsorship marketing.

Sponsorship marketing occurs when the company pays money to sponsor someone or some group that is participating in an activity.
(Easy; p. 422)

83) Describe event marketing.

Event marketing is similar to a sponsorship, except that it is in support of a specific event, such as a rodeo or county fair.
(Easy; p. 424)

84) What is a trade regulation?

A trade regulation is a finding or a ruling that implicates an entire industry in a case of deceptive or unfair marketing practices.
(Easy, p. 419)

85) What are the three key public relations' functions?

1. Monitor internal and external publics.
2. Provide positive information to each public.
3. React quickly to any shift by any of the publics from the desired position.

(Moderate; p. 403)

86) Who are the major external stakeholders for a public relations department to consider?

- Channel members
- Customers
- The media
- The local community
- The financial community
- Government
- Special-interest groups

(Moderate; pp. 405-407)

87) What are the major public relations tools?

- Newsletters
- Internal media (bulletin board, e-mail, letters, memos)
- Media news releases
- Stockholder correspondence
- Annual reports
- Special events
- Collaboration with internal publics

(Moderate; p. 414)

88) What criteria must be met to deem an advertisement deceptive or misleading?

1. A substantial number of people, or the typical person, is left with a false impression or misrepresentation that relates to the product.
2. The misrepresentation induces people or the "typical person" to make a purchase.

(Moderate; p. 416)

89) Identify the typical steps in an FTC investigation sequence from the initial complaint to a decision that is appealed to the Supreme Court.

1. Consent order
2. Administrative complaint
3. Cease-and-desist order
4. Full commission
5. U.S. Court of Appeals
6. U.S. Supreme Court

(Challenging; p. 418)

90) Discuss the various damage control strategies that can be used by a firm.

Reactive strategies are designed to counter the negative action that has occurred. The reactive strategies include crisis management, apology, defense of innocence, excuses, justifications, and other explanations. Proactive strategies are designed to promote goodwill for the firm or to prevent negative publicity. Proactive strategies include entitling, enhancements, and Internet interventions.

(Challenging; pp. 410)

CHAPTER 14
INTERNET MARKETING

True-False Questions

1) E-commerce is selling goods or services on the Internet.
   (True; Easy; p. 439)

2) A flashy Web site designed to attract attention is created when the primary goal is advertising.
   (True; Easy; p. 439)

3) Cyberbait is a lure or type of attraction designed to bring people to a Web site.
   (True; Easy; p. 442)

4) FAQ stands for Follow-After-Questionnaire, designed to strengthen understanding of e-commerce customers.
   (False; Easy; p. 439)

5) A growing area of e-commerce in the business-to-business sector is on-line exchanges and auctions.
   (True; Easy; p. 444)

6) One of the advantages of e-commerce over brick-and-mortar stores is the ability to reach consumers around the globe.
   (True; Easy; p. 446)

7) Brand spiraling is the practice of using interactive media to promote and attract consumers to an on-line Web site.
   (False; Easy; p. 450)

8) Business-to-business marketers were among the first companies to actually make profits using the Internet.
   (True; Moderate; p. 437)

9) The three incentives that must be present for consumers to consider a purchase online are financial incentives, convenience incentives, and price incentives.
   (False; Moderate; p. 441)

10) An example of a value-added incentive is personalization.
    (True; Moderate; p. 443)

11) In routine rebuy situations, purchasing agents can go to the Internet to compare prices and product information.
    (True; Moderate; p. 443)

12)   Many of the online exchanges and auctions are neutral companies that simply match
        buyers and sellers.
            (True; Moderate; p. 444)

13)   Cyberbranding is a brand loyalty-building technique.
            (False; Moderate; p 450)

14)   Many experts believe that traditional Internet banner ads have little influence on
        shoppers.
            (True; Moderate; p. 448)

15)   While the Internet makes it possible to have customers from anywhere in the world,
        almost 46% of current Internet customers turn away international orders because they do
        not have processes in place to fill the international orders.
            (True; Challenging; p. 446)

16)   One component that is not required or necessary on an e-commerce site is a catalog.
            (False; Challenging; p. 441)

17)   Web sites, similar to displays at retail stores, can be rearranged to create excitement and
        interest, but basic links and location of merchandise should not be changed too often.
            (True; Challenging; p. 442)

18)   While the Victoria's Secret Internet Fashion Show associated with the Super Bowl was a
        major success, due to the number of people who were drawn to the site, failure to tell the
        IT department resulted in the site crashing from too many trying to access it.
            (True; Challenging; p. 448)

19)   Word-of-mouth advertising is a form of brand spiraling where consumers pass along
        positive information about the brand.
            (False; Challenging; p. 450)

20)   Viral marketing is a form of interactive marketing.
            (False; Challenging; p. 456)

Multiple-Choice Questions

21)   E-Bay CEO Meg Whitman considers E-Bay to be _____ .
            a) a replacement for bricks and mortar operations
            b) a global marketplace
            c) slowly losing ground to Amazon.com
            d) largely unfazed by the September 11 attacks
        (b; Easy; p. 434)

22)	Internet Web sites can serve all of the following functions, except _____ .
    a)	advertising
    b)	sales support
    c)	shopping cart
    d)	customer service
(c; Easy; p. 438)

23)	FAQ stands for _____ .
    a)	frequently answered questions
    b)	frequently asked questions
    c)	frequently asked queries
    d)	follow-up answer questionnaire
(b; Easy; p. 439)

24)	When goods are sold on the Internet, the approach to marketing is known as _____ .
    a)	retail by e-mail
    b)	viral marketing
    c)	e-commerce
    d)	vicarious shopping
(c; Easy; p. 439)

25)	Which is not a necessary component of an e-commerce site?
    a)	catalog
    b)	shopping cart
    c)	payment method
    d)	video stream
(d; Easy; p. 440)

26)	A shopping cart is used for _____ .
    a)	making inquiries
    b)	asking questions
    c)	placing an order
    d)	returning merchandise
(c; Easy; p. 440)

27)	A catalog is used for _____ .
    a)	displaying merchandise
    b)	placing orders
    c)	answering questions
    d)	providing information about other companies
(a; Easy; p. 440)

28) Visa and MasterCard have recently created ads about _____ .
    a) payment systems with a high level of security
    b) placing orders
    c) creating better catalogs
    d) changing purchasing habits
(a; Easy; p. 441)

29) Which is still a reason that some shoppers are reluctant to make Internet purchases?
    a) price
    b) quality
    c) security
    d) convenience
(c; Easy; p. 440)

30) E-commerce incentives do not include _____ .
    a) quality incentives
    b) financial incentives
    c) convenience incentives
    d) value-based incentives
(a; Easy; p. 441)

31) A financial incentive can include all of the following except _____ .
    a) consumer promotion
    b) introductory price
    c) home delivery
    d) e-coupon
(c; Easy; p. 441)

32) When a business checks on the status of an order, looks up shipment information or reviews billing data, the business is taking advantage of which incentive?
    a) financial
    b) convenience
    c) value
    d) shopping
(b; Easy; p. 442)

33) Cyberbait is a form of _____ .
    a) financial incentive
    b) consumer incentive
    c) convenience incentive
    d) value incentive
(a; Easy; p. 442)

34) Value-added incentives include _____ .
    a) billing data
    b) shipment information
    c) U-pons or coupons
    d) shopping cart
(c; Easy; p. 443)

35) Business-to-business Web sites are visited more often _____ .
    a) when there is off-line advertising and sales promotion
    b) during non-business hours
    c) before a trade show
    d) when Internet advertising is high
(a; Easy; p. 449)

36) Cyberbranding is _____ .
    a) integrating on-line and off-line branding tactics
    b) a form of brand equity
    c) a form of spamming
    d) a form of virus
(a; Easy; p. 450)

37) Using traditional media to promote and attract customers to a Web site is _____ .
    a) spamming
    b) brand spiraling
    c) consumer incentive
    d) value-added marketing
(b; Easy; p. 450)

38) Sending out unsolicited e-mail ads is called _____ .
    a) spamming
    b) viral marketing
    c) consumer sales support
    d) personalized marketing
(a; Easy; p. 455)

39) The halo effect is _____ .
    a) a well-received brand leads customers to try purchasing goods and services over the Internet
    b) that people like a particular Web site and go there more often
    c) that people like salespeople who are pleasant
    d) that consumers only shop when the banner is enticing
(a; Easy; p. 451)

40) Interactive marketing is _____ .
   a) individualizing and personalizing Internet messages
   b) spamming
   c) creating a catalog
   d) designing a shopping cart
   (a; Easy; p. 456)

41) The person who manages the firm's Web site is called _____ .
   a) the marketing manager
   b) the creative
   c) the web master
   d) the web creator
   (c; Easy; p. 452)

42) The Auction for America on-line program to support victims of the September 11 attacks
   was hosted by _____ .
   a) e-Bay
   b) Amazon.com
   c) AOL
   d) Target.com
   (a; Moderate; p. 435)

43) Which of the following statements is not true concerning the Internet?
   a) over 25% of all business-to-business purchases are placed through some type of
      Internet connection
   b) business-to-business advertising is increasing on the Internet
   c) by 2004, 30% of business-to-business advertising dollars will be spent on the
      Internet
   d) Internet retail sales account for almost 2.5% of all retail sales (c; Moderate; p.
      437)

44) If a consumer were trying to discern additional information, he or she may go to _____ .
   a) the front page
   b) a banner
   c) the FAQ screen
   d) the shopping cart
   (c; Moderate; p. 439)

45) Besides security issues, the primary reason why some consumers do not shop on-line is
   _____ .
   a) it requires a new purchasing habit
   b) they do not have the time
   c) they don't think they can find what they want
   d) they are overwhelmed by the number of choices
   (a; Moderate; p. 440)

46) Using a fantasy football league to market additional products is a form of _____ .
   a) viral marketing
   b) bait and switch
   c) cyberbait
   d) convenience incentive
   (c; Moderate; p. 442)

47) Which would not be cyberbait?
   a) special loss-leader offer
   b) tips on some subject
   c) a game to be played online
   d) a FAQ screen
   (d; Moderate; p. 442)

48) A financial incentive may cause a consumer to switch to e-commerce; a value-added incentive is designed to _____ .
   a) changing purchasing habits more permanently
   b) create brand awareness
   c) substitute payment plans
   d) find new buyers
   (a; Moderate; p. 443)

49) A new business-to-business e-commerce site would have the easiest time encouraging businesses to utilize the new site with _____ .
   a) new task purchases
   b) rebuy purchases
   c) modified rebuy situations
   d) small product purchases
   (b; Moderate; p. 443)

50) Internet e-commerce does not use _____ .
   a) financial incentives
   b) convenience incentives
   c) value-added incentives
   d) mark-up incentives
   (d; Moderate; p. 441)

51) While e-commerce can increase international orders, many are turned away because _____ .
   a) the company does not understand the culture
   b) the company is focused on domestic business
   c) the company does not have a process in place to fill the order
   d) the company is highly prejudiced
   (c; Moderate; p. 446)

52)   Which is not a problem in International e-commerce?
      a) software compatibility
      b) band-width
      c) language and meaning
      d) a strong brand is not an advantage due to the number of competitors
(d; Moderate; p. 446)

53)   Posting a firm's Web address on a bag used to package goods sold at a bricks and mortar store is a form of _____ .
      a) brand reinforcement
      b) brand spiraling
      c) interactive marketing
      d) virtual marketing
(b; Moderate; p. 450)

54)   Brand spiraling is _____ .
      a) an on-line advertising technique
      b) an off-line advertising technique
      c) a manufacturing technique
      d) a technical improvement
(b; Moderate; p. 450)

55)   Which is not true concerning brand loyalty in e-commerce?
      a) it is the same as being a heavy user
      b) consumers believe the brand is superior
      c) consumers have positive affective feelings toward the company
      d) brand loyal consumers make purchases for reasons beyond price and convenience
(a; Moderate; p. 451)

56)   Which is the least effective?
      a) regularly changing the front page of a Web site
      b) spamming
      c) interactive marketing
      d) viral marketing
(b; Moderate; pp. 455-456)

57)   A consumer would get a personalized message from the Internet company using which Internet methodology?
      a) spamming
      b) viral marketing
      c) interactive marketing
      d) individualized marketing
(c; Moderate; p. 456)

58) Which of the following is tied to e-mail?
   a) interactive marketing
   b) catalog
   c) viral marketing
   d) multimedia marketing
(c; Moderate; p. 456)

59) Viral marketing is _____ .
   a) spamming
   b) a form of interactive marketing
   c) preparing an ad tied to an e-mail containing an endorsement
   d) using a virus to spread a marketing message
(c; Moderate; p. 456)

60) Problems with Web site design do not include _____ .
   a) clueless banners
   b) slow-loading front pages
   c) too many screens
   d) FAQs
(d; Moderate; p. 458)

61) Internet companies gain a major advantage because _____ .
   a) they reach senior citizens so effectively
   b) they save 10% to 20% of their sales, marketing, and distribution costs
   c) they help the company compete using a new distribution
   d) they do not require advertising to gain brand recognition
(b; Challenging; p. 438)

62) The e-commerce component most directly affected by security concerns is _____ .
   a) interstitial advertising
   b) the catalog
   c) the shopping cart
   d) payment programs
(d; Challenging; pp. 440-441)

63) Persuading a first-time buyer is best achieved using _____ .
   a) interstitial advertising
   b) financial incentives
   c) convenience incentives
   d) value-based incentives
(b; Challenging; pp. 441-442)

64) A hotel knows a customer often stays for a week and offers that person a discount for booking online. This is an example of _____ .
   a) merchandising
   b) a financial incentive
   c) a convenience incentive
   d) a value-added incentive
(d; Challenging; p. 443)

65) Business-to-business straight rebuys online are attractive due to _____ .
   a) personalized messages
   b) financial incentives
   c) convenience incentives
   d) value-added incentives
(c; Challenging; p. 442)

66) One advantage of e-commerce in the business-to-business area is _____ .
   a) wide visibility
   b) reduced costs of sales calls and commissions
   c) the ability to eliminate the sales department
   d) reduced costs at trade shows
(b; Challenging; p. 444)

67) Which is false concerning interstitial ads?
   a) They are also called pop-up ads.
   b) They are controversial.
   c) They have high intrusion value.
   d) They do not work as well as traditional banner ads.
(d; Challenging; p. 448)

68) Brand spiraling would not take place on _____ .
   a) television
   b) radio
   c) a billboard
   d) a mall kiosk
(d; Challenging; p. 450)

69) The halo effect has an impact on _____ .
   a) Internet hits
   b) sales of new products and services
   c) brand parity
   d) interstitial ad recall
(b; Challenging; p. 451)

70) Which is <u>not</u> true concerning cyberbait?
   a) It is a form of convenience incentive.
   b) It can be a lottery or contest.
   c) It can be a consumer promotion tactic.
   d) It should be changed on a regular basis.
(a; Challenging; p. 442)

71) Spamming is the Internet equivalent of _____ .
   a) direct marketing by mail
   b) advertising on television
   c) promotion at a trade show
   d) public relations and cause-related events
(a; Challenging; p. 455)

72) Interactive marketing creates _____ .
   a) a personalized banner on a Web page
   b) personalized Web and e-mail campaigns
   c) personalized message by telemarketing
   d) personalized interstitial advertisements
(b; Challenging; p. 456)

73) Viral marketing relies on _____ .
   a) a series of click-throughs
   b) use of FAQs
   c) highly visible banners
   d) word-of-mouth communications
(d; Challenging; p. 456)

74) Since they do not take title to goods, most business-to-business online exchange and auction sites earn their revenue by _____ .
   a) charging sellers a fee to advertise
   b) charging sellers a fee to list their merchandise
   c) charging a percentage fee on each transaction that occurs
   d) charging buyers a fee to register and purchase products
(c; Challenging; p. 444)

75) While consumers and businesses use the Internet for shopping, there are some who want to make the actual purchase at a physical store or business location. To meet this need, many e-commerce companies _____ .
   a) use software, such as Vicinity, that will provide store locations with maps
   b) do not provide actual prices so buyers will be encouraged to go to the store
   c) offer a lower price if a consumer will purchase on the Internet and allow the company to drop ship the merchandise
   d) will not allow buyers to make the actual purchase online
(a; Challenging; p. 444)

76) The most difficult challenge e-commerce companies face in the international market is
    _____ .
    a) the language barrier
    b) a lack of companies that can ship large or bulky products to other countries
    c) the inferior infrastructure in many countries
    d) the technical side of e-commerce, specifically software incompatibility
    (d; Challenging; p. 446)

77) In terms of Web site design, a cultural disaster to avoid in international e-commerce
    would be _____ .
    a) using white background and graphics in Asia, Europe and Latin America
    b) a waving hand in Middle East countries
    c) showing a woman with exposed arms or legs in the Middle East
    d) using a dog as a company logo in France
    (c; Challenging; p. 446)

78) All of the following are methods that will drive people to a new Internet site. However,
    the method that is used the most, by 38% of the respondents, is _____ .
    a) Internet content search
    b) word-of-mouth communications
    c) Internet banner
    d) television ad
    (a; Challenging; p. 448)

79) The luster of using e-mails to send business advertisements has worn off with over 70%
    of recipients saying they are receiving too many e-mail ads and 55% saying they delete
    the ads without ever looking at them. As an alternative, many business-to-business
    companies have shifted to _____ .
    a) viral marketing
    b) interactive marketing
    c) b-to-b newsletters
    d) cyberbait
    (c; Challenging; p. 449)

80) In terms of customer service, the primary advantage to customers in using the vendor's
    Web site for customer service is _____ .
    a) ability to purchase additional products
    b) speed and efficiency of obtaining information and placing orders
    c) availability of FAQs
    d) the accuracy of shipping orders
    (b; Challenging; p. 453)

Short-Answer Questions

81)   What basic marketing functions can be performed on the Internet?

- Advertising
- Sales support
- Customer service
- Public relations
- E-commerce

(Easy; p. 438)

82)   What are the three components of an e-commerce site?

1. A catalog
2. A shopping cart
3. A payment system

(Easy; p. 440)

83)   What two consumer issues must be overcome to get them to make an on-line purchase?

Security issues and purchasing habits
(Easy; p. 440)

84)   What kinds of e-commerce incentives can be offered to encourage consumers to purchase products over the Internet?

- Financially-based incentives
- Convenience-based incentives
- Value-based incentives

(Easy; p. 441)

85)   What is brand spiraling?

The practice of using traditional media to promote and attract consumers to a Web site.
(Easy; p. 450)

86)   What is interactive marketing?

Using the Internet to individualize and personalize Internet Web content and e-mail messages.
(Easy; p. 456)

87)   What is viral marketing?

Preparing an advertisement that is tied to e-mail.
(Easy; p. 456)

88) What IMC activities are related to Internet programs?

- Branding and brand loyalty
- Sales support
- Customer service
- Consumer promotions

(Moderate; p. 449)

89) What design issues can lead to poor Web sites?

- Clueless banners
- A slow-loading front page
- Forcing people to go through numerous screens
- Too much verbal information
- Too many technical terms
- Hard to navigate sites

(Challenging; p. 458)

90) How can the Internet be used to provide sales support for a company's sales force?

- Provide information about clients and prospects
- Provide information about products that a salesperson can relay to a potential buyer
- Provide past purchase history of current customers
- Provide information on a prospect's organization

(Challenging; pp. 452-453)

CHAPTER 15
IMC FOR SMALL BUSINESSES AND ENTREPRENEURIAL VENTURES

True-False Questions

1) All small businesses and new ventures are essentially the same.
(False; Easy; p. 467)

2) A corporate spinoff or start up is an intrepreneurship.
(True; Easy; p. 467)

3) Finding a target market for a new small business requires a match of consumer needs, goods or services, and finding a unique niche.
(True; Easy; p. 469)

4) Guerilla marketing involves using traditional marketing tools to reach consumers with a controversial message.
(False; Easy; p. 473)

5) Finding grass roots contact points, such as rock concerts, garage sales or car races, is known as lifestyle marketing.
(True; Easy; p. 476)

6) Buying from a new vendor or purchase risk is not typically a major problem for a new company.
(False; Easy; p. 468)

7) A consumer who is loyal to a small business and provides word-of-mouth endorsements for that firm is known as an advocate.
(True; Easy; p. 480)

8) The Pasta House Company's frequency program is similar to a McDonald's gift certificate because the Pasta House's frequency coupon can be redeemed at any location.
(False; Moderate; p. 464)

9) The difference between a small business and an entrepreneurship is that the small business has a goal of rapid growth.
(False; Moderate; p. 467)

10) One key to defining consumer needs for a new business is to understand which desirable good or service is not currently available to a specific group.
(True; Moderate; p. 469)

11) When the goal of a company is to find a way to stand alone in the marketplace, the company is seeking to identify a unique selling position.
   (True; Moderate; p. 470)

12) Marketing funds for small firms are spent in the same ways as multinationals, such as Proctor and Gamble.
   (False; Moderate; p. 474)

13) One method small businesses can use to gain greater exposure from advertising dollars is to explore cooperative advertising programs with manufacturers.
   (True; Moderate; p. 477)

14) Lifestyle marketing is different from guerilla marketing because guerilla marketing does not include special events or shows.
   (False; Moderate; pp. 473-476)

15) A group of medical professionals who form a company with specific objectives, such as risk management, is known as an intrepreneurship consortium.
   (False; Challenging; p. 467)

16) When a child psychologist advertises that she specializes in cases of children who have experienced trauma or stress, her organization has established a unique selling position.
   (True; Challenging; p. 470)

17) A new restaurant, which provides "buy one meal, get one free" coupons, is attempting to reduce purchase risk.
   (True; Challenging; p. 480)

18) Traditional marketing is more likely to require imagination and energy where guerilla marketing identifies success using sales as a measure.
   (False; Challenging; p. 474)

19) A new fertilizer featured in a booth at a farmer's market is an example of advocate marketing.
   (False; Challenging; pp. 474-475)

20) Magazines are widely used to market small businesses.
   (False; Challenging; p. 478)

21) The Pasta House Company is an example of _____ .
   a) an entrepreneurial venture
   b) an intrepreneurship
   c) a small business
   d) lifestyle marketing
(a; Easy; pp. 464-467)

22) A corporate spinoff or start up is _____ .
   a) an entrepreneurship
   b) an intrepreneurship
   c) corporate altruism
   d) vertical integration
(b; Easy; p. 467)

23) A family-owned dry cleaners that has no intention of expanding to any more locations is _____ .
   a) an entrepreneurship
   b) intrepreneurship
   c) a small business
   d) guerilla marketing
(c; Easy; p. 467)

24) Which is not typically a challenge to a new small business?
   a) advocates passing along negative word of mouth
   b) advertising and promotional clutter
   c) small budgets for marketing and advertising
   d) consumers who are not aware of the company
(a; Easy; p. 468)

25) One key for a small business owner to understand and define consumer needs is to _____.
   a) spend time in a corporate setting first
   b) ignore demographics and concentrate on psychological tendencies
   c) identify what a particular group desires that is not currently available
   d) ignore consumer names and concentrate on demographics
(c; Easy; p. 469)

26) Small business owners must match a niche with _____ .
   a) a large demographic
   b) consumer needs as well as the good or service
   c) currently available advocates
   d) past purchasing patterns of big spenders
(b; Easy; p. 468)

27) A feature, which allows a newly formed company to stand alone and be distinct, is a
_____.
   a) form of marketing myopia
   b) entrepreneurship by-line
   c) individualized selling place
   d) unique selling position
(d; Easy; p. 470)

28) A new firm should devote a minimum of how much of its revenues to marketing programs?
   a) one to two percent
   b) three to five percent
   c) 10 percent
   d) 15 percent
(b; Easy; p. 472)

29) Using low-cost, creative strategies to reach customers is known as _____ .
   a) traditional marketing
   b) incentive marketing
   c) media planning
   d) guerilla marketing
(d; Easy; p. 473)

30) Which is the best option for a small business?
   a) network television
   b) prime time television, but local
   c) rotated cable spots
   d) ignoring television and using other media
(c; Easy; p. 477)

31) Which is true concerning radio and small businesses?
   a) it is too expensive
   b) national ad time is readily available
   c) it is possible to reach business buyers and other members of a buying center
   d) drive time offers the lowest cost for spots
(c; Easy; pp. 477-478)

32) Attending a Chamber of Commerce meeting to find new customers is an example of
_____ .
   a) intrusive connections
   b) lifestyle marketing
   c) networking
   d) traditional marketing
(c; Easy; p. 479)

33) Using coupons, samples, price discounts and free first visits are examples of _____ .
  a) reducing purchasing risk
  b) expensive marketing programs small business cannot afford
  c) lifestyle marketing
  d) guerilla marketing
(a; Easy; p. 480)

34) A person who is loyal to a business and draws others through word of mouth is _____ .
  a) an advocate
  b) an adventurer
  c) a first user
  d) a liability reducer
(a; Easy; p.480)

35) One of the fast-growing market segments is _____ .
  a) ethnic markets
  b) teenagers
  c) women
  d) Caucasians
(a; Moderate p. 473)

36) Traditional methods for helping customers reach a small business do not include _____ .
  a) telephone calls
  b) mail
  c) in-store visits
  d) billboard advertisement
(d; Moderate; p. 479)

37) Which is associated with traditional marketing rather than guerilla marketing?
  a) measure success by sales
  b) measure success by profits
  c) based on psychology and human behavior
  d) aims messages at individuals and small groups
(a; Moderate; p. 474)

38) Which is associated with guerilla marketing rather than traditional marketing?
  a) measure success by sales
  b) grows by adding customers
  c) grows through existing customers and referrals
  d) aims messages at large groups
(c; Moderate, p. 474)

39) The following concepts are associated with guerilla marketing, <u>except</u> _____ .
   a) requires energy and imagination
   b) designed to obliterate the competition
   c) aims messages at individuals and small groups
   d) "you marketing," based on how we can help "you"
(b; Moderate; p. 474)

40) When the Pasta House Company gives a coupon for free food following previous purchases, it is an example of _____ .
   a) neighborhood marketing
   b) a frequency program
   c) incentive purchasing
   d) company altruism
(b; Moderate; p. 464)

41) Genuity.com was a wireless phone and Internet service started by a long-distance carrier, making it _____ .
   a) an entrepreneurial venture
   b) an intrepreneurship
   c) a small business
   d) a takeover or merger
(b; Moderate; p. 467)

42) A family-owned car dealership passed from father to son is an example of _____ .
   a) entrepreneurship
   b) intrepreneurship
   c) a small business
   d) a spin-off
(c; Moderate; p. 467)

43) All of the following are typical problems for new businesses, <u>except</u> _____ .
   a) strong brand equity
   b) advertising and promotional clutter
   c) consumers who are cautious of the new good or service
   d) worries about negative word of mouth
(a; Moderate; p. 468)

44) Which does <u>not</u> belong?
   a) niche
   b) good/service
   c) agency
   d) need
(c; Moderate; p. 468)

45) VIPdesk, a wireless concierge service, has a _____ .
   a) brand recognition problem
   b) unique selling position
   c) corporate competitor advantage
   d) economies of scale problem
(b; Moderate; p. 470)

46) Which would be the least advisable name for a new business?
   a) Acme Products
   b) Champion Dry Cleaners
   c) Margie's Herbal Shoppe
   d) Computer Solutions
(a; Moderate; p. 470)

47) Identifying a market niche best matches _____ .
   a) corporate and brand image
   b) consumer buyer behaviors
   c) business-to-business buyer behaviors
   d) promotions opportunity analysis
(d; Moderate; p. 471)

48) Using Spanish-speaking endorsers in advertisements for a company targeting Hispanics is an example of _____ .
   a) lifestyle marketing
   b) guerilla marketing
   c) personalizing the product and message
   d) a generic appeal
(c; Moderate; p. 473)

49) A paintball "cat shoot" (at a painting of a cat) designed to raise funds for the local humane society while attracting attention and customers, is an example of _____ .
   a) guerilla marketing
   b) lifestyle marketing
   c) brand recognition development
   d) poor marketing judgment due to alienating customers
(a; Moderate; p. 473)

50) A new business owner who tries to obliterate the competition and generate sales through advertising expenditures is using _____ .
   a) traditional marketing
   b) guerilla marketing
   c) safe marketing tactics
   d) lifestyle marketing
(a; Moderate; p. 474)

51) The primary objective of a small business sponsorship program should be to _____ .
a) reach a wide audience
b) make sure the right people are exposed to the company
c) eliminate expenses
d) create brand parity
(b; Moderate; p. 475)

52) When Flip Records gives free tapes of new music to people in specialty stores, tattoo parlors, and at rock concerts, the firm is using _____ .
a) an incentive program
b) targeted give aways
c) lifestyle marketing tactics
d) traditional marketing tactics
(c; Moderate; p.476)

53) The best time for a radio spot for a small business, funds permitting, is _____ .
a) rotated
b) drive time
c) mid evening
d) late evening
(b; Moderate; p. 478)

54) Low CPM and long-term exposure for a small business can be accomplished using
_____.
a) newspaper
b) radio
c) billboard
d) magazine
(c; Moderate; p. 478)

55) In terms of guerilla marketing, which of the following is an excellent method of reaching customers and also an excellent method for customers to reach the company?
a) traditional advertising
b) lifestyle marketing
c) advocate programs
d) billboards
(b; Moderate; p. 479)

56) Database management, direct marketing, and quality personal selling can turn customers into _____ .
a) advocates
b) allies
c) endorsers
d) experts
(a; Moderate; p. 480

57) Which is not true about direct marketing?
a) According to the Direct Marketing Association, each dollar spent on direct marketing yields $10.00 in sales.
b) It should begin with defining the goals of the program and then specifying an audience.
c) It is rarely viable for small businesses due to the large expense.
d) The principles that guide direct marketing are also useful for e-mail, telephone, and fax campaigns.
(c; Moderate; p. 481)

58) Which is not true regarding trade and consumer promotions?
a) They include using specialty advertising, such as pens or calendars, to increase consumer recognition and loyalty.
b) Trade promotions are not effective for small manufacturers.
c) They are most effective when tied to a database program in some way.
d) They should reflect the firm's image and position.
(b; Moderate; p. 481)

59) Which is most oriented to aggressive growth?
a) entrepreneurship
b) intrepreneurship
c) small business
d) a corporate spin-off
(a; Challenging; p. 467)

60) Which is most oriented to providing steady income for the owner?
a) entrepreneurship
b) intrepreneurship
c) small business
d) a corporation
(c; Challenging; p. 467)

61) Which is the common denominator for all new businesses?
a) They all seek aggressive growth.
b) They all try to provide a solid income for the owners.
c) They are all unknown in the marketplace.
d) They rarely experience purchase risk.
(c; Challenging; p. 467)

62) A new business owner and the company's advertisers should focus on which of these product aspects?
a) compatibility
b) benefits
c) features
d) flexibility
(b; Challenging; p. 468)

63) Customer needs are <u>not</u> determined by _____ .
   a) demographic characteristics
   b) psychological tendencies
   c) benefits which have not been previously obtainable
   d) feelings about product liability
(d; Challenging; p. 470)

64) When defining a product, it is important to outline what the product will do and _____ .
   a) what it won't do
   b) what it might do
   c) what it should do
   d) what it often does
(a; Challenging; p. 470)

65) Why is The Pasta House Company a better name than Geeks on Call?
   a) people like pasta more than geeks
   b) Geeks on Call suggests a 24/7 service
   c) one creates a clearer perception of what the company offers
   d) one is more creative than the other
(c; Challenging; p. 470)

66) Which two elements match consumer needs in a target market analysis?
   a) corporate image and consumer buyer behaviors
   b) consumer buyer behaviors and business-to-business buyer behaviors
   c) business-to-business buyer behaviors and promotions opportunity analysis
   d) corporate image and promotions opportunity analysis
(b; Challenging; p. 471)

67) Creating an IMC plan for a new small business ordinarily does <u>not</u> focus on _____ .
   a) finding the right creative to make commercials
   b) locating customers
   c) making it easy for customers to reach the company
   d) reducing purchase risk for consumers
(a; Challenging; p. 472)

68) Who created the guerilla marketing concept?
   a) Jay Livingstone
   b) Conrad Hilton
   c) the Marlboro company and Philip Morris
   d) Jay Conrad Levinson
(d; Challenging; p. 473)

69) Which is least likely to be a guerilla marketing tactic?
- a) radio spots during drive time
- b) participation in a trade show
- c) involvement in sponsorships
- d) use of alternative media

(a; Challenging; p. 474)

70) Typical goals for trade shows do <u>not</u> include _____ .
- a) generating leads
- b) setting prices for the upcoming year
- c) introducing a new good or service
- d) generating awareness of the company

(b; Challenging; pp. 474-475)

71) To maximize impact, a logical tie-in for a small business sponsorship would be _____ .
- a) magazine advertising
- b) trade shows
- c) a public relations program
- d) buyer incentives such as price-off deals

(c; Challenging; p. 475)

72) When a "legalize marijuana" group distributes literature and free key chains at a rock concert, the group is engaging in _____ .
- a) lifestyle marketing
- b) an illegal act
- c) a sponsorship program
- d) public relations' activities

(a; Challenging; p. 476)

73) Advertising in newspapers is most advisable for a small business with a(n) _____ .
- a) teenage target market
- b) Generation X target market
- c) ethnic target market
- d) baby boomer target market

(d; Challenging; p.478)

74) An attorney who is willing to give a speech about legal rights at a Rotary Club meeting and then speak with individual members of a Kiwanis club meeting is engaging in _____.
- a) guerilla marketing
- b) networking
- c) a sponsorship program
- d) proactive target marketing

(b; Challenging; p. 479)

75) In choosing a name for a new business, if a name is chosen, such as Geeks on Call, that does not clearly tell consumers what product is being sold, the company will _____ .
   a) have to expend extra effort in defining the business so customers will know what is being sold
   b) need to develop a tagline that tells customers what is being sold
   c) have to develop a more precisely defined market niche
   d) have to spend more money on sales promotions to encourage customers to try the product
(a; Challenging; p. 470)

76) Guerilla marketing is _____ .
   a) the best method for locating customers for a small business
   b) not so much a method of marketing as a mentality or approach to marketing
   c) a method a small business can use to obliterate the competition
   d) based on a database marketing foundation
(b; Challenging; p. 474)

77) A furniture store setting up a special display of massage chairs at a little league baseball tournament is an example of _____ .
   a) generating leads
   b) developing a unique market niche
   c) lifestyle marketing
   d) creating a clearly defined product
(c; Challenging; p. 476)

78) For a new business that is relatively unknown, the primary objective of advertising should be _____ .
   a) to generate leads
   b) to create brand awareness
   c) to persuade consumers to choose the new business
   d) to remind consumers where the business is located
(b; Challenging; pp. 477)

79) Newspaper advertising will likely be the most effective for a small business when _____ .
   a) full page ads are used
   b) the ad is on Sunday or Wednesday
   c) the ad defines clearly the new product or businesses USP
   d) the ad is tied to a consumer promotion and encourages consumer action
(d; Challenging; p. 478)

80) For a new startup business, the most cost-effective method of keeping customers and turning them into advocates is through _____ .
   a) database management
   b) direct marketing
   c) consumer promotions
   d) personal selling
(a; Challenging; p. 480)

Short-Answer Questions

81) What are the three steps in analyzing a market?

   1. Understand and define consumer needs
   2. Establish a clearly defined good or service
   3. Develop a unique market niche
(Easy; p. 469)

82) What is a unique selling position (USP)?

   Some feature which allows a newly formed company to stand out and be distinct from other competitors.
(Easy; p. 470)

83) Name and describe the three most common forms of small business.

   1. Entrepreneurship in which a company is being formed with the express goal of becoming larger through an aggressive growth agenda.
   2. Intrepreneurship, which is a corporate spinoff or start up.
   3. A small business, which is normally family owned, or is a consortium of professionals with specific goals in mind.
(Moderate; p. 467)

84) What are the common challenges new businesses face?

   - Consumers who are not aware of the company
   - Consumers who are cautious or wary of trying a new product, service or company
   - Advertising and promotional clutter
   - Small budgets for marketing, advertising, and promotional activities
   - They are the most vulnerable to negative word of mouth
(Moderate; p. 468)

85) What three activities are crucial parts of an IMC plan for a new small business?

1. Locating customers
2. Making it easy for customers to reach the new company
3. Reducing purchase risk for customers

(Moderate; p. 472)

86) What is lifestyle marketing?

It is a form of guerilla marketing. The goal is to locate customers in targeted places of interest that reflect their lifestyles, such as bluegrass festivals, farmers' markets, stock car races, 5k runs, and other identifiable activities.

(Moderate; p. 476)

87) How is the Internet used in marketing a new small business?

The Internet should link the company's site to places such as the Chamber of Commerce page, city home page or visitor's bureau. All other advertisements and marketing activities should mention the company's Web site and address.

(Moderate; p. 478)

88) How can customers reach a new small business?

- Through traditional methods such as a telephone, Internet or mail address
- By managers networking in the community
- Through lifestyle marketing
- With interactions on a Web site

(Moderate; pp. 479-480)

89) What methods are available to help a new business reduce purchase risk?

- Samples
- Coupons
- Price discounts
- Referral discounts
- Free first consultation visits
- Money-back guarantees

(Moderate; p. 480)

90) What is guerilla marketing? How is it different from traditional marketing?

Guerilla marketing is focusing on low-cost, creative strategies to reach the right people.

It is different from traditional marketing because the company uses energy and imagination; measures success through profits rather than sales; bases efforts on psychology and human behavior rather than experience; seeks growth through existing

customers and referrals rather than by simply trying to add customers; aims messages at targeted, rather than large groups; and focuses on the customer rather than the company. Primary places to implement guerilla tactics include trade shows, sponsorship programs, public relations' programs, and by using alternative media.
(Challenging; pp. 473-474)

CHAPTER 16
EVALUATING AN INTEGRATED MARKETING PROGRAM

True-False Questions

1) When studying marketing effectiveness, evaluation techniques involving respondent behaviors are numbers-based.
    (True; Easy; p. 490)

2) When studying marketing effectiveness, evaluation techniques that study messages are numbers-based.
    (False; Easy; p. 490)

3) A storyboard is a series of pictures providing an overview of the structure of an ad.
    (True; Easy; p. 492)

4) Attitude and opinion studies may be used to evaluate sales promotion devices, such as direct mail pieces.
    (True; Easy; p. 499)

5) The only criterion for judging advertising effectiveness is increased sales.
    (False; Easy; p. 505)

6) It is difficult, if not impossible, to measure redemption rates of coupons, premiums, and direct mail pieces.
    (False; Easy; p. 508)

7) Emotional reaction tests are self-report instruments.
    (True; Easy; p. 500)

8) Message evaluation programs assess both cognitive and peripheral cues in an ad.
    (True; Moderate; p. 490)

9) Concept testing is aimed at behavioral responses to ads, such as purchases or redemption rates.
    (False; Moderate; p. 493)

10) Focus groups are usually made up of 8-10 people who are representative of a target market.
    (True; Moderate; p. 493)

11) Comprehension tests are designed to see if subjects recall seeing a marketing piece in the past 24 hours.
    (False; Moderate; p. 498)

12) A portfolio test is a form of copytesting.
   (True; Moderate; p. 494)

13) Open-ended questions narrow down a study to specific items the researcher wishes to test.
   (False; Moderate; p. 499)

14) A psychogalvanometer measures a person's eye movements.
   (False; Moderate; p. 501)

15) Emotional reaction tests are a form of copytesting.
   (False; Challenging; p. 500)

16) A theater test can be used to study a print ad from a billboard or the side of a bus.
   (False; Challenging; p. 494)

17) A pupillometric meter is designed to study emotional arousal.
   (True; Challenging; p. 502)

18) PACT was designed to assist in the evaluation of television ads.
   (True; Challenging; p. 503)

19) Market share is one measure of success of an overall IMC program.
   (True; Challenging; p. 513)

20) Social responsibility should focus solely on eliminating negative activities, such as false ads.
   (False; Challenging; p. 514)

Multiple-Choice Questions

21) An examination of a creative message and the physical design of an advertisement or other marketing communication pieces are called _____ .
   a) respondent behavior evaluation
   b) pretesting
   c) message evaluation
   d) message synthesis
   (c; Easy; p. 490)

22) A message evaluation can take place _____ .
   a) when an ad is completed
   b) when an ad has been shown to the public
   c) when the campaign is complete
   d) at any stage of the development of an ad
   (d; Easy; p. 492)

23) A storyboard is used to outline the structure of _____ .
   a) a radio ad
   b) a television ad
   c) a television program
   d) print ads
   (b; Easy; p. 492)

24) Concept testing examines _____ .
   a) the success of an IMC program
   b) the media purchasing pattern the agency will use
   c) the art in an ad
   d) the ad content and the impact of the content on customers
   (d; Easy; p. 493)

25) When 8-10 people test an ad concept because they are representative of a target market, they are called _____ .
   a) a pre- and post-test group
   b) a review group
   c) an analysis group
   d) a focus group
   (d; Easy; p. 493)

26) Which would help a moderator understand why an intended message in an ad was not correctly understood by an individual or group?
   a) a comprehension test
   b) a reaction test
   c) a behavioral response test
   d) a translation test
   (a; Easy; p. 494)

27) Which would help a moderator understand why an intended message received a negative response?
   a) a comprehension test
   b) a reaction test
   c) an analytical test
   d) a psychogalvanometer
   (b; Easy; p. 494)

28) Which copytesting method below is used with print ads?
   a) a portfolio test
   b) a theater test
   c) a regulatory test
   d) a pupillometer
   (a; Easy; p. 494)

29) Which copytesting method is used with television ads?
    a) a portfolio test
    b) a theater test
    c) a reaction test
    d) the mall intercept technique
(b; Easy; p. 494)

30) DAR stands for _____ .
    a) Delivery of Advertising Response
    b) Data Analysis and Review
    c) Day-After Recall
    d) Data Analysis of Advertising Reactions
(c; Easy; p. 495)

31) For recall tests, when consumers are prompted about a product category, it is part of a(n) _____ .
    a) unaided recall test
    b) aided recall test
    c) concept testing model
    d) mall intercept technique
(b; Easy; p. 495)

32) When individuals are given copies of an ad and asked if they recognize it or have seen it before, the technique is called _____ .
    a) an aided recall test
    b) a storyboard test
    c) a theater test
    d) a recognition test
(d; Easy; p. 497)

33) A 1 = highly favorable to 7 = highly unfavorable scale is called _____ .
    a) a recognition test
    b) a closed-ended questionnaire
    c) an open-ended questionnaire
    d) a validation test
(b; Easy; p. 499)

34) Warmth monitors and the Discover Why Internet program are examples of _____ .
    a) emotional reaction tests
    b) recall tests
    c) recognition tests
    d) physiological arousal tests
(a; Easy; p. 500)

35) Which uses a computer joystick to test emotional reactions to an ad?
    a) a warmth monitor
    b) a psychogalvanometer
    c) a pupillometric test
    d) voice-pitch analysis
(a; Easy; p. 500)

36) Psychogalvanometers, pupillometric tests, and voice-pitch analysis are forms of _____ .
    a) emotional reaction tests
    b) recall tests
    c) recognition tests
    d) physiological arousal tests
(d; Easy; p. 501)

37) Which measures perspiration levels?
    a) a warmth monitor
    b) a psychogalvanometer
    c) a pupillometric test
    d) a sweat meter
(b; Easy; p. 501)

38) Which is not a behavioral evaluation approach?
    a) actual sales
    b) coupon redemptions
    c) emotional arousal
    d) Internet hits
(c; Easy; p. 505)

39) Test markets are typically not used to measure _____ .
    a) advertising effectiveness
    b) pricing tactics
    c) brand equity
    d) new product acceptance
(c; Easy; pp. 510-511)

40) A purchase simulation test takes place in a _____ .
    a) mall
    b) retail store
    c) laboratory
    d) theater
(c; Easy; pp. 511-512)

41) Which of the following is a short-term measure of marketing effectiveness?
   a) sales and redemption rates
   b) brand loyalty and equity
   c) product-specific awareness
   d) awareness of the overall company
   (a; Moderate; p. 491)

42) Which item listed below is not studied using concept tests?
   a) sales rates
   b) the meaning of a message
   c) a translation of an international ad
   d) the value associated with a prize
   (a; Moderate; p. 493)

43) Which is not part of the Position Advertising Copytesting approach?
   a) the procedure should be relevant to the advertising objective being tested
   b) researchers should agree on how results will be used
   c) the test should measure the degree of social responsibility
   d) researchers should use multiple measures to evaluate ads
   (c; Moderate; p. 503)

44) Which measures both negative and positive feelings about a marketing piece?
   a) a comprehension test
   b) a reaction test
   c) an emotional test
   d) a recognition test
   (b; Moderate; p. 494)

45) Which copytesting test does not involve mixing in the marketing piece with other pieces that are not being evaluated?
   a) a portfolio test
   b) a warmth meter
   c) a theater test
   d) the mall intercept technique
   (b; Moderate; pp. 494, 500)

46) The mall intercept technique can incorporate a copytesting procedure known as a _____ .
   a) warmth meter
   b) pupillometer
   c) psychogalvanometer
   d) portfolio test
   (d; Moderate; p. 494)

47) Which of the following statements is true in both aided and unaided recall tests?
   a) Incorrect responses are important data.
   b) Older people recall ads more easily.
   c) They are used in conjunction with behavioral measures.
   d) They are less effective than other evaluative tests.
   (a; Moderate; p. 496)

48) For recognition tests, which is least likely to affect the ability of respondents to recognize an advertisement?
   a) the size of the ad
   b) the customer uses the product already
   c) the ad seemed interesting
   d) a regular person is the spokesperson in the ad
   (d; Moderate; p. 498)

49) Emotional reaction tests, such as warmth meters, are _____ .
   a) focused on recall
   b) designed to measure recognition
   c) self-report tests
   d) intrusive tests
   (c; Moderate; p. 501)

50) Emotional responses measured by instruments that are not self-report programs are called _____ .
   a) recall tests
   b) recognition tests
   c) cognitive accumulation tests
   d) physiological arousal tests
   (d; Moderate; p. 501)

51) Which measures pupil dilation to test emotional reactions to an ad?
   a) an eye meter
   b) a pupillometer
   c) a visualization meter
   d) a focus test
   (b; Moderate; p. 502)

52) Using a pupillometer, pupils become smaller when the subject reacts?
   a) positively
   b) negatively
   c) slowly
   d) vocally
   (b; Moderate; p.502)

53)   In a voice-pitch test, which would indicate greater emotion?
        a) higher pitched response
        b) lower range response
        c) shorter response
        d) the subject's gender
(a; Moderate; p. 502)

54)   The test used to see if an ad changed the consumer's mind about a product is called

        _____ .
        a) a warmth meter
        b) a recognition test
        c) a recall test
        d) persuasion analysis
(d; Moderate; p. 502)

55)   Which is not part of the PACT approach?
        a) The ad should be based on a theory of human response.
        b) The ad should receive a single exposure to measure results.
        c) The ads shown should be at the same stage of development.
        d) The sample should represent the larger population.
(b; Moderate; p. 503)

56)   Which does not affect the evaluation of an advertisement?
        a) a delayed impact of the ad
        b) consumers changing their minds while in the store
        c) the consumer price index changes
        d) brand equity considerations
(c; Moderate; p. 507)

57)   Which is used to study the effectiveness of point-of-purchase displays?
        a) the PACT approach
        b) the POPAI approach
        c) the multi-cultural model
        d) the WEST approach
(b; Moderate; p. 508)

58)   Which uses "cookies" to track behavioral responses?
        a) response cards
        b) toll-free number calls
        c) Internet responses
        d) coupon redemptions
(c; Moderate; p. 509)

59) Test markets are <u>not</u> used to _____ .
    a) study promotions and premiums
    b) test emotional reactions to an ad in a shopping mall
    c) set prices
    d) study new product acceptance
(b; Moderate; p. 510)

60) Which statement below, concerning purchase stimulation tests, is false?
    a) They are performed in laboratory settings.
    b) They measure opinions and attitudes.
    c) They are a form of pre and posttest.
    d) They are designed to resemble a shopping experience.
(b; Moderate; pp. 511-512)

61) Which method below is <u>not</u> a method for evaluating public relations programs?
    a) counting clippings
    b) calculating the number of impressions
    c) using the advertising equivalence technique
    d) counting Internet hits
(d; Moderate; p. 512)

62) In a public relations evaluation, the advertising equivalence technique is designed to measure _____ .
    a) the number of advertising clippings compared to news releases
    b) the number of subscribers and buyers of a print medium in which the company's name has been mentioned
    c) the number of calls to a toll-free number following a public relations event, coupled with an advertising campaign
    d) calculating the cost of the time and space if a story were an advertisement
(d; Moderate; p. 513)

63) Which is an affective response to a marketing message?
    a) sales and redemption rates
    b) product specific awareness
    c) awareness of the overall company
    d) liking the company
(d; Challenging; p. 491)

64) Which of the following evaluation methods simulates clutter?
    a) a comprehension test
    b) a reaction test
    c) a theater test
    d) a behavioral response test
(c; Challenging; p. 494)

65) Which test would McDonald's use to see if consumers remembered an ad for a new sandwich?
   a) DAR
   b) PACT
   c) POPAI
   d) test market
(a; Challenging; p. 495)

66) Which test would tell McDonald's that consumers formed a negative impression of a sandwich after seeing an ad?
   a) a comprehension test
   b) an attitude or opinion test
   c) a recall test
   d) a behavioral reaction test
(b; Challenging; p. 499)

67) Which group is least likely to recall an ad for a soft drink?
   a) children
   b) teens
   c) baby boomers
   d) senior citizens
(d; Challenging; p. 496)

68) Which evaluation method below is not a self-report test?
   a) a warmth meter
   b) an emotional reaction test
   c) a closed-ended questionnaire
   d) a voice-pitch analysis
(d; Challenging; p. 501)

69) Using a pupillometric meter, seeing offensive sexual content in an ad would make a person's pupils _____ .
   a) dilate or become larger
   b) become smaller
   c) be interrupted by blinking
   d) become unfocused due to tears
(b; Challenging; p. 502)

70) Discussing an ad for tampons, which a consumer found to be offensive, would cause the person's voice to become _____ .
   a) more shrill
   b) softer
   c) louder
   d) lower
(a; Challenging; p. 502)

71) Which term below means generalizable to other groups?
   a) valid
   b) reliable
   c) practical
   d) universal
   (a; Challenging; p. 505)

72) Which measures the effectiveness of point-of-purchase displays?
   a) the mall intercept technique
   b) coupon redemptions
   c) the PACT approach
   d) the POPAI approach
   (d; Challenging; p. 508)

73) For evaluating public relations, which technique involves knowing the circulation and newsstand sales of a paper?
   a) counting clippings
   b) calculating impressions
   c) the advertising equivalence technique
   d) the multiple exposure method
   (b; Challenging; pp. 512-513)

74) Which is the least used, but probably best method, for evaluating P.R.?
   a) counting clippings
   b) calculating impressions
   c) advertising equivalence
   d) comparison to objectives
   (d; Challenging; p. 513)

75) Cajun Pizza has a new idea for an advertising campaign. However, before developing the ad, they would like to see how consumers would react. The appropriate evaluation technique would be a _____ .
   a) concept test
   b) copytest
   c) recognition test
   d) attitude or opinion test
   (a; Challenging; p. 493)

76) Media Research has decided to call 200 people to ask them about ads for banks and what they could remember about each ad. All of the following items would be appropriate for testing for recall, except _____ .
   a) theme music
   b) length of the television ad, i.e. 15 second, 30 second, 45 second
   c) primary selling point
   d) cost of the item
   (a; Challenging; p. 502)

77) When both recognition tests and recall tests are used, the average recall score tends to be approximately _____ .
   a) 0.32 times the average recognition score
   b) equal to the average recognition score
   c) 1.5 times higher than the average recognition score
   d) 3 times higher than the average recognition score
(a; Challenging; p. 498)

78) For evaluating advertisements, such as a Maidenform ad with a woman at an airport dressed only in her underwear, respondents may give what they consider to be a socially acceptable response instead of their true feelings. In such situations, the best evaluation method would be _____ .
   a) persuasion analysis
   b) emotional reaction tests
   c) physiological arousal tests
   d) attitude and opinion tests
(c; Challenging; p. 502)

79) McCormick wants to test three different advertisements for its new Chicken Dijon gravy before it launches the product nationwide . To measure actual market reaction, McCormick's best approach would be to _____ .
   a) use the ads in three different markets and use DAR tests to measure the impact
   b) use different test markets for each of the three ads and compare the actual sales differences among the three markets
   c) place the three ads in a theater test and measure the audience reaction
   d) count the number of times the brand name or specific product is mentioned in the media after each ad has run
(b; Challenging; p. 510)

80) In evaluating marketing communications, scanner data are helpful in which of the following evaluation methods?
   a) test markets
   b) recall tests
   c) purchase simulation tests
   d) mall intercept copytests
(a; Challenging; pp. 507, 510-511)

Short-Answer Questions

81) What are the three main forms of copytesting?

   1. Portfolio tests
   2. Theater tests
   3. The mall intercept technique
(Easy; p. 494)

82) What are the two main forms of Day-After Recall tests?

1. Aided recall
2. Unaided recall
(Easy; p. 495)

83) What forms of emotional reaction tests are available?

- Warmth meter
- Psychogalvanometer
- Pupillometric test
- Voice-pitch analysis
(Easy; p 500)

84) What makes measuring the effectiveness of advertisements more problematic?

- The influence of other factors, such as the weather
- The delayed impact of an ad
- Consumers changing their minds while in the store
- Whether or not the brand is in the consumer's evoked set
- Brand equity considerations
(Moderate; p. 507)

85) What behavioral measures of advertising effectiveness are possible?

- Sales figures
- Calls to a toll-free number
- Response cards
- Internet responses
- Redemption rates of coupons and premiums
- Contest and sweepstakes' entries
- Responses to direct mail pieces
(Moderate; pp. 505-506)

86) What can test markets assess?

- Advertisements
- Promotions and premiums
- Pricing tactics
- New products
(Moderate; p. 510)

87)   What four methods are available for evaluating public relations' activities?

1. Counting clippings
2. Calculating the number of impressions
3. The advertising equivalence technique
4. Comparison to PR objectives
(Moderate; pp. 515-513)

88)   What objectives can be used to measure the overall IMC program?

- Market share
- Innovation
- Productivity
- Physical and financial resources
- Profitability
- Manager performance and development
- Employee performance and attitudes
- Social responsibility
(Challenging; pp. 513-515)

89)   What components of a marketing communications plan can be evaluated using concept tests?

- The copy or verbal component
- The message and its meaning
- The translation of copy in an international ad
- The effectiveness of peripheral cues
- The value associated with an offer or prize in a contest
(Challenging; p. 493)

90)   What items should be identified when evaluating an advertising program?

- Short-term outcomes, such as sales
- Long-term results, such as brand loyalty
- Product-specific awareness
- Awareness of the overall company
- Affective responses, such as a positive brand image
(Challenging; p. 491)